Jordan L. Harding

WINDOW ON CYPRUS

P.I.O
Press and Information Office
Republic of Cyprus
www.moi.gov.cy/pio

Second Edition 2007

Design by: Nicos Ierodiaconou/Andros Georgiou
Printed by: Imprinta ltd
Edited by: Soterios Stavrou
Elengo Frangoulidou

Cover by: Christos Avraamides

Editorial Assistance by: Riana Magidou

The publishers of this book wish to express their
gratitute to all those who have contributed to the
fulfilment of this project.

P.I.O 431/2007 - 5000
ISBN 978-9963-38-487-7

CONTENTS

Unless otherwise noted, the material in this book was compiled by goverment staff

Petra tou Romiou where legend says that goddess Aphrodite emerged from the waves

Cyprus, Island of Aphrodite

Cyprus is known as the birthplace of Aphrodite, the ancient Greek goddess of love and beauty. Accounts concerning her origins vary. According to Hesiod, she was born when Cronus, the son of Uranus (sky) and Gaea (earth), castrated his father with a sickle and tossed the severed genitals into the sea which began to foam. From the *aphros* (foam) emerged the goddess on the south west coast of the island near the town of Pafos at a place called Petra tou Romiou.

Homer provides a different genealogy of Aphrodite. As he would have it, Gaea was born of Chaos, and Uranus was born of Gaea. Their two offspring, Cronus and Rhea, married and brought forth Zeus. In turn, Zeus and Dione were the parents of Aphrodite. Aphrodite was married to Hephaistus, the lame god of the forge. According to mythology, Aphrodite's passionate love affair with her brother Ares, the god of war, produced three sons and a daughter. So disgraced were both deities in the eyes of the rest of the gods that eventually Aphrodite fled Greece and found a new home on Cyprus.

Myths are part of the fabric of society and may at times provide clues to events. Many a scholar have used myths as stepping stones in their search of the historical past. In the case of Aphropdite, archaeological findings have revealed aspects of the goddess which differ from those attributed to her by Greek mythology. What is certain is that throughout antiquity Cyprus was one of the most important places, if not the most famous, where Aphrodite was worshipped. There were many sanctuaries on the island dedicated to her, the most famous in Pafos, at a place called *Omphalos* (navel), which was considered to be on an equal footing with Delphi.

Aphrodite of Cyprus was not merely the blonde goddess of love, grace and beauty who indulged in amorous whims, as often depicted in simplistic mythology. She was also an ancient divinity with origins linked to the worship of the powers of life; a goddess of fertility of oriental origins who was worshipped on the island since the Iron Age, and whom the Cypriots presumably did not at

Marble statue of Aphrodite from Soli, first century B.C., Cyprus Museum
PHOTO: PRESS AND INFORMATION OFFICE

Petra tou Romiou

that time call Aphrodite; a local divinity who was adopted by the Greeks when they arrived on the island and who was renamed Aphrodite, when Greek culture began to strongly influence local religion during the fifth century B.C.; a divinity whose cult was maintained on the island for centuries, even while Christianity was spreading.

From the scripts of ancient Greek poets and mythological tradition to contemporary Cypriot culture, Aphrodite has been almost synonymous with Cyprus. Whether known as Kypris (the Cyprian), or Pafia (named after the town of Pafos), the goddess has been above all a Cypriot goddess, permeating Cypriot life through the ages. Even today, the name Aphrodite is widely used for girls on the island; it is also the brand name of a popular Cyprus wine.

Sanctuary of Apollo Hylates, Kourion, Roman Period

History

A Long Journey

The history of Cyprus is one of the oldest recorded in the world. From the earliest times, Cyprus' historical significance far outweighed its small size. Its strategic position at the crossroads of three continents and its considerable resources of copper and timber combined to make it a highly desirable territorial acquisition.

The first signs of civilisation date to the ninth millennium B.C., but it was the discovery of copper (3900 – 2500 B.C.) that was to bring wealth and trade to the island. Around 1200 B.C., a process began that was to largely stamp the island with the national identity that it still has today. The arrival of Mycenaean-Achaean Greeks as permanent settlers brought with them their language and culture. Cyprus was subsequently subjugated by various conquerors; nevertheless, it managed to retain its Greek identity. The Turkish Cypriots came much later. They were mostly the descendants of the Ottoman Turks, who occupied the island for more than three hundred years (1571-1878) and have contributed their own heritage to the country.

Christianity was introduced to the island during the first century A.D. by St. Paul and St. Barnabas, founder of the Church of Cyprus.

Khirokitia Neolithic settlement, a well-organised community of stone domed dwellings

PHOTO: PRESS AND INFORMATION OFFICE

Chronology

Neolithic Period (8200-3900 B.C.)

Remains of the oldest known settlements in Cyprus date from this period. They can best be seen at Khirokitia, just off the Nicosia to Limassol highway. At first, only stone vessels were used. Pottery appeared in a second phase after 5000 B.C.

Protome of a cat made of andesite from Pareklisia - «Shyllourokambos», tenth millenium B.C.
Photo: Cyprus Museum

Chalcolithic Age (3900-2500 B.C.)

A transitional period between the Stone Age and the Bronze Age. Most Chalcolithic settlements were found in western Cyprus where a fertility cult developed. Copper was discovered and was beginning to be exploited on a small scale.

Terracota sanctuary model, Red Polished ware from Kotchati, c. 2000 B.C.
Photo: Cyprus Museum

Bronze Age (2500-1050 B.C.)

Copper was more extensively exploited bringing wealth to Cyprus. Trade developed with the Near East, Egypt and the Aegean where Cyprus was known under the name of Alasia.

Red and Black Polished clay bowls, Early Bronze Age, from Vounous(*)[1]
Photo: Cyprus Museum

After 1400 B.C., Mycenaeans from Greece began to come to the island as merchants. Around 1200 B.C., mass waves of Achaean Greeks came to settle on the island and established the first city-kingdoms of Pafos, Salamis, Kition and Kourion. The hellenisation of the island was in progress.

Faience rhyton from Kition, Late Brozne Age, thirteenth century B.C.
Photo: Cyprus Museum

Clay tablet from Kalavassos inscribed in the Cypro-Minoan script, thirteenth century B.C.
Photo: Press and Information Office

[1]*References to sites, monuments and artifacts in the Turkish occupied areas of Cyprus are marked with an asterisk (*) throughout the book*

Geometric Period (1050-750 B.C.)

Cyprus had ten Greek city-kingdoms. The cult of Aphrodite flourished, and Phoenicians settled at Kition in the ninth century B.C. The eighth century B.C. was a period of great prosperity.

The ancient city - kingdom of Soli (*)
Photo: Press and Information Office

Aerial view of the theatre, gymnasium and baths at ancient Salamis (*)
Photo: Demetrios Michaelides

Archaic and Classical Period (750-310 B.C.)

Prosperity continued, but the island fell prey to several conquerors. Cypriot kingdoms were ruled by a succession of foreign cultures: after the Assyrians came the Egyptians and then the Persians. King

The stadium at Kourion
Photo: Cyprus Museum

Evagoras of Salamis (who ruled from 411-374 B.C.) unified Cyprus and made the island one of the leading political and cultural centres of the Greek world.

The city-kingdoms of Cyprus welcomed Alexander the Great, King of Macedonia, and Cyprus became part of his empire.

Gold earrings in the shape of a sitting sphinx, fourth-fifth century B.C.
Photo: Press and Information Office

General view of the gymnasium at Salamis (*)
Photo: Cyprus Museum

Hellenistic Period (310-30 B.C.)

After the rivalries for succession between Alexander's generals, Cyprus eventually came under the Hellenistic state of the Ptolemies of Egypt and from then on belonged to the Greek Alexandrine world. The Ptolemies abolished the city-kingdoms and unified Cyprus. Pafos became the capital.

Limestone portait of Alexander the Great from Soli(*), 325-150 B.C.
Photo: Cyprus Museum

Roman Period (30 B.C.– 330 A.D.)

Cyprus came under the dominion of the Roman Empire. During the missionary journey of Apostles Paul and Barnabas, the Proconsul Sergius Paulus was converted to Christianity, and Cyprus became the

Over-lifesize bronze statue of the Roman Emperor Septimius Severus, 193-211 A.D., found at the village of Kythrea (*), now in the Cyprus Museum
Photo: Press and Information Office

first country to be governed by a Christian. Destructive earthquakes occurred during the first century B.C. and the first century A.D. and cities needed to be rebuilt. In 313 the Edict of Milan granted religious freedom in the Roman Empire, and Cypriot bishops attended the Council of Nicaea in 325.

Floor mosaic at the House of Dionysos, Pafos, third century A.D.
Photo: Press and Information Office

Byzantine Period (330 - 1191 A.D.)

After the split of the Roman Empire, Cyprus came under the Eastern Roman Empire, subsquently known as Byzantium, with Constantinople as its capital. Christianity became the official religion. New earthquakes during the fourth century A.D. completely destroyed the main cities of the island. Once again, new cities arose. Constantia, built near the site of ancient Salamis, became the capital, and large basilicas were built during the fourth and fifth centuries.

In 488 Emperor Zeno granted the Church of Cyprus full autonomy and gave the archbishop the privileges of holding a sceptre instead of a pastoral staff, wearing a purple mantle and signing in red ink. After an initial invasion by the Arabs in 647, the island was for three centuries Cyprus under constant attacks by Arabs and pirates until 965, when Emperor Nicephoros Phocas expelled the Arabs from Asia Minor and Cyprus.

The Byzantine Church of Panayia tis Asinou, eleventh-twelfth century
Photo: Christos Violaris

The Byzantine Church of Panayia Chrysopolitissa, built in the thirteenth century over the ruins of the largest Early Byzantine Basilica on the island.
Photo: Christos Violaris

Kolossi castle, built by the Knights of St. John of Jerusalem during the crusades.

Photo: Cyprus Tourism Organisation

Richard the Lionheart and the Knights Templar (1191 - 1192)

Isaac Comnenus, a Byzantine governor and self- proclaimed emperor of Cyprus, behaved discourteously toward survivors of a shipwreck involving ships of King Richard's fleet on their way to the Holy Lands during the Third Crusade. Among the survivors were Richard's sister Joanna, Queen of Sicily, and his betrothed Berengaria of Navarre. Richard in revenge fought Isaac, defeated him, took possession of Cyprus and married Berengaria of Navarre in Limassol, where she was crowned Queen of England.

A year later, Richard sold the island for 100 000 dinars to the Knights Templar, a Frankish military order, who resold it at the same price to Guy de Lusignan, deposed King of Jerusalem.

Frankish (Lusignan) Period (1192 - 1489)

Cyprus was ruled on the feudal system. The Catholic Church officially replaced the Greek Orthodox, which, though under severe suppression, managed to survive. The city of Famagusta was then one of the richest in the Near East. It was during this period that the historical names of Lefkosia, Ammochostos and Lemesos were

St. Hilarion castle on Pentadaktylos Range(*)
Photo: Press and Information Office

Pafos castle at the west end of the harbour
Photo: Press and Information Office

changed to Nicosia, Famagusta and Limassol, respectively. The era of the Lusignan dynasty ended when Queen Catherine Cornaro ceded Cyprus to Venice in 1489.

Famagusta Gate of the Nicosia Venetian Walls, with the interior rooms and the passage way used today as a cultural centre
Photo: Press and Information Office

Venetian Period (1489 - 1571)

Venetians viewed Cyprus as the last bastion against the Ottomans in the Eastern Mediterranean and fortified the island, tearing down lovely buildings in Nicosia to reduce the boundaries of the city within fortified walls. They also built impressive walls around Famagusta which were considered at the time as state of the art military architecture.

The Othello Tower and the Lion of Venice, Famagusta Walls
Photo: Press and Information Office

The Church of Ayia Sophia turned into a mosque, in the occupied part of Nicosia
Photo: Press and Information Office

Street in Nicosia, end of the nineteenth century
Photo: J.P. Foscolo (end 19th century)

Ottoman Occupation (1571 - 1878)

In 1570 Ottoman troops attacked Cyprus, captured Nicosia, slaughtered twenty thousand of the population and laid siege to Famagusta for a year. After a brave defence by Venetian commander Marc Antonio Bragadino, Famagusta fell to Lala Mustafa Pasha, who at first allowed the besieged a peaceful exodus, but later ordered the flaying of Bragadino. On annexation to the Ottoman Empire, Lala Mustafa Pasha became the first governor. The Ottoman Turks, whose descendants together with the descendants of Muslim converts of mainly Latin origin, form today the largest part of the Turkish Cypriot community, were to rule Cyprus until 1878. During the Ottoman period, the Muslim minority eventually acquired a Cypriot identity. Initially, the Greek Orthodox Church was granted a certain amount of autonomy, the feudal system was abolished and the freed serfs were allowed to acquire land. They were, however, heavily taxed. As the power of the Ottoman Turks declined, their rule became increasingly brutal and corrupt. In many instances Greek and Turkish Cypriots struggled together against the oppression of Ottoman rule. It was with a certain amount of optimism—which proved to be sadly misplaced—for union of Cyprus with Greece that British rule was welcomed.

British Rule (1878 - 1960)

Under the 1878 Cyprus Convention, the Ottoman Turks handed over the administration of the island to Britain in exchange for guarantees that Britain would protect the crumbling Ottoman Empire against possible Russian aggression. It remained formally part of the Ottoman Empire until the latter entered World War I on the side of Germany, and Britain in consequence annexed the island in 1914. In 1923 under the Treaty of Lausanne, Turkey relinquished all rights to Cyprus, which in 1925 was declared a Crown colony. In 1940 Cypriot volunteers massively joined the British Armed Forces and served with them throughout World War II.

Women's bazaar in Nicosia, end of the nineteenth century
Photo: J.P. Foscolo

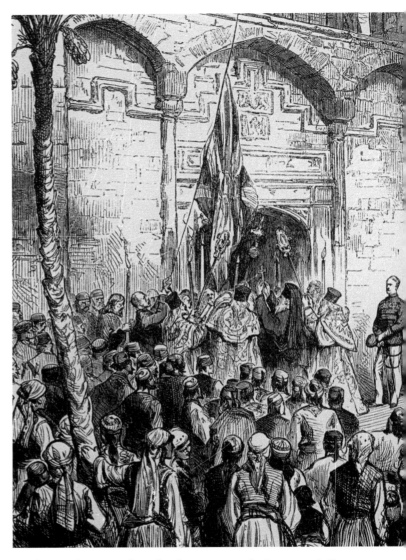

Hopes for self-determination in the post-war period were shattered by the British, who considered the island vitally strategic, especially after the debacle of Suez in 1956. If the island became part of Greece, as was the wish of the Greek Cypriots, Britain would lose its bases and influence in the area. Applying a policy of divide and rule, Britain rekindled Turkey's interest in Cyprus. Ankara could not countenance a Greek island so close to its southern border. Britain used the Turkish Cypriots, who constituted 18 percent of the population, as counterweight in their fight against the Greek Cypriots and deliberately involved Turkey, which for the first time began to advance the idea of partition of the island.

The Cyprus problem, as the tug of war for the future of the island came to be known, has its roots in foreign interference and occupation. For

Greek Orthodox priests blessing the British flag at the Kykko Metoch, Nicosia, in the presence of the High Commissioner
Wood engraving, Illustrated London News, 1878

The first British High Commissioner, Sir Garnet Wolseley, receiving Turkish notables in the Konak on the occasion of Bairam
Wood engraving, Illustrated London News, 1879

centuries, Cyprus was occupied by one power or another but through it all kept its predominantly Hellenic character and Christian Orthodox traditions. The ambition for enosis (union) with Greece was already strong when Greece won its own independence from the Ottomans early in the nineteenth century. When Britain became the ruler of the island, the hope that this dream could become reality intensified. After all peaceful means had been exhausted, a national liberation struggle was launched in 1955 against colonial rule and for union with Greece.

The liberation struggle ended in 1959 with the Zurich-London agreements signed by Britain, Greece and Turkey as well as representatives of the Greek and Turkish Cypriots, leading to Cyprus' independence.

The last Governor of Cyprus Sir Hugh Foot, Archbishop Makarios and Dr Fazil Kutchuk sign the Treaty of Establishment of the Republic of Cyprus, 16 August 1960

Photo: Press and Information Office

Republic of Cyprus - 1960

As a result of the Zurich-London agreements, Cyprus became an independent republic on 16 August 1960. According to the above treaty, Britain retained two sovereign bases (158.5 square kilometres) on the island, at Dekeleia and Akrotiri-Episkopi.

The 1960 constitution incorporated a system of entrenched minority rights for Turkish Cypriots unparalleled in any other country. The 18 percent Turkish Cypriot community was offered a privileged position in the state institutions of Cyprus (Turkish Cypriot vice-president, three out of the ten ministers of the government and fifteen out of fifty seats in the House of Representatives). The Turkish Cypriot leadership's use of its extensive powers of veto brought about a deadlock and political paralysis. In November 1963, when Cyprus' first president, Archbishop Makarios, put forward proposals for amendment to the constitution in order to facilitate the smooth functioning of government, the Turkish side promptly rejected them, arguing that the constitution could not be amended without the entire independence agreement being revoked.

The Turkish Cypriot ministers withdrew from the Council of Ministers, and Turkish Cypriot civil servants ceased attending their offices. The ensuing constitutional deadlock gave rise to intercommunal clashes and Turkish threats to invade.

The Cyprus government did all in its power to restore the situation to normalcy. It offered economic encouragement to Turkish Cypriots, who in the meantime had been forced by the Turkish Cypriot

Greek Cypriot soldiers taken prisoners by the Turkish invading troops
Photo: Press and Information Office

Turkish troops land on the coast of Keryneia, 20 July 1974
Photo: Press and Information Office

leadership to abandon their homes and settle in exclusively Turkish enclaves, to return to their hometowns. And in 1968 the government initiated intercommunal talks with the Turkish Cypriot leadership under UN auspices for a negotiated agreement on a more functional constitutional system for Cyprus.

By 1974 some progress was achieved through the intercommunal talks but developments that summer interrupted this process with devastating consequences for Cyprus.

Turkish Invasion and Occupation

On 15 July 1974, the ruling military junta of Greece staged a coup to overthrow the democratically elected government of Cyprus. On 20

Destruction caused by the by the Turkish Air Force bombing, August 1974

Photo: Press and Information Office

July, Turkey, using the coup as a pretext, invaded Cyprus, purportedly to restore constitutional order. Instead, it seized about 36.2 percent of the territory of the island in the north, an act universally condemned as a gross infringement of international law and the UN Charter. Turkey, only 75 kilometres away, had repeatedly claimed, for decades before the invasion and frequently afterwards, that Cyprus was of vital strategic importance to it. Ankara has since defied a host of UN resolutions demanding the withdrawal of its occupation troops from the island.

Homeless Greek Cypriot refugees after the 1974 Turkish invasion

Photo: Press and Information Office

The invasion and occupation had disastrous consequences. About 200 000 Greek Cypriots living in the north, nearly one quarter of the population of Cyprus, were forcibly expelled from the occupied northern part of the island where they constituted 80 percent of the population. These people are still deprived of the right to return to their homes and properties. A further 20 000 Greek Cypriots enclaved in the occupied areas were gradually, through intimidation and denial

of their basic human rights, forced to abandon their homes. Today, there are around 500 enclaved persons (Greek Cypriots and Maronites).

The invasion also had a disastrous impact on the Cyprus economy, because 30 percent of the economically active population became unemployed and because of the loss of:

- 70 percent of the gross output
- 65 percent of the existing tourist accommodation capacity
- 87 percent of new hotels under construction
- 83 percent of general cargo handling at the Famagusta port
- 40 percent of school buildings
- 56 percent of mining and quarrying output
- about 41 percent of livestock production
- 48 percent of agricultural exports
- 46 percent of industrial production.

Furthermore, Turkish forces occupied an area which accounted for 46 percent of crop production and much higher percentages in the production of citrus fruit (79 percent), cereals (68 percent), tobacco (100 percent), carobs (86 percent) and green fodder (65 percent).

About fifteen hundred Greek Cypriot civilians and soldiers disappeared during and after the invasion. Many had been arrested and some of them seen in prisons in Turkey and Cyprus before their disappearance. The fate of all but a handful remains unknown. To resolve this humanitarian issue, it is essential to have Turkey's cooperation, which so far has not been forthcoming.

Greek Cypriot refugees living in tents after the 1974 Turkish invasion

Photo: Press and Information Office

Relatives of the missing looking at photos of their loved ones

Turkey has also promoted demographic changes in the occupied territory through the implantation of Anatolian settlers. Since the invasion, some 160 000 Turks from Turkey have been illegally imported into the occupied areas.

The large influx of settlers has negatively affected the living conditions of the Turkish Cypriots. Poverty and unemployment has forced over fifty-five thousand to emigrate. At the present, Turkish Cypriots are estimated as making up only 11 percent of the native population.

Forty-three thousand Turkish soldiers, equipped with the latest weapons and supported by the Turkish air force and navy, are still in the occupied areas. According to the UN Secretary-General's Report (December 1995), the occupied areas are "one of the most densely militarised areas in the world."

Destruction of Cultural Heritage

Turkey and the illegal regime in the occupied areas have pursued a deliberate policy aimed at plundering and destroying the ancient cultural and historical heritage of Cyprus. This policy is part of a wider goal to turkify the island and erase all evidence of its Cypriot character.

Abundant evidence gathered from foreign and Turkish Cypriot press, as well as from other authoritative sources demonstrates the magnitude of the damage and destruction.

As a consequence of Turkey's policy and illegal actions:

- at least fifty-five churches have been converted into mosques
- another fifty churches and monasteries have been converted into stables, stores, hostels or museums, or have been demolished
- the cemeteries of at least twenty-five villages have been desecrated and destroyed
- innumerable icons, religious artifacts and all kinds of archaeological treasures have been stolen and smuggled abroad
- illegal excavations and smuggling of antiquities continue with the involvement of the occupying forces
- Greek place names have been illegally changed to Turkish ones.

The Republic of Cyprus is making great efforts to recover stolen items which include invaluable icons, frescoes, mosaics, texts and artifacts. A successful case of repatriation involved the sixth century mosaics that were illegally removed from the Church of Panayia Kanakaria in the occupied areas and sold to an art dealer in the U.S.A. Following a legal battle that attracted world attention, the U.S. Courts ruled that the mosaics should be returned to their legal owner, the Church of Cyprus.

In contrast to the total disrespect shown to Greek and Greek Orthodox cultural heritage by the occupation regime, all Muslim sites in the area controlled by the government of Cyprus are, as a matter of official policy, properly and respectfully preserved and maintained.

On 15 November 1983, the Turkish-occupied area was unilaterally declared an independent "state." Through UN Security Council Resolutions 541 of 1983 and 550 of 1984, the international

The desecrated Armenian Monastery of Saint Magar Sourp on the Pentadaktylos Range(*)
Photo: Press and Information Office

The pillaged cemetery next to the Church of Ayia Varvara in the village of Akanthou (*)
Photo: Press and Information Office

The Church of Ayios Mamas, in Morfou(*)   Photo: Press and Information Office

The Church of Ayios Georgios, Karpassia peninsula (*), as seen after the 1974 Turkish invasion   Photo: Press and Information Office

community condemned this unilateral declaration by the Turkish Cypriot regime, declared it both illegal and invalid, and called for its immediate revocation. To this day, no other country except Turkey has recognised this spurious entity.

Negotiations for a solution to the Cyprus problem have been going on intermittently since 1975 under the auspices of the United Nations. A settlement is sought on the basis of the UN Security Council resolutions on Cyprus and two high-level agreements concluded between the Greek and Turkish Cypriot leaders in 1977 and 1979.

In an effort to enhance the prospects for a settlement and safeguard the security of all Cypriots, the government of Cyprus had formally proposed the total demilitarisation of the island. The proposal envisaged the withdrawal of the Turkish occupying forces, as well as the disbanding of the Cyprus National Guard and the "Turkish Cypriot Armed Forces". All weapons and military equipment would be turned over to the UN Peace-Keeping Force in Cyprus (UNFICYP). UNFICYP would have the right of inspection to ascertain compliance with these measures. Turkey has refused to consider the proposal and continues to maintain its illegal military presence on the island.

The Cyprus Problem – Latest Developments

In the aftermath of the 1974 invasion of Cyprus by Turkey, there were intermittent talks toward negotiating a solution to the Cyprus problem. From 1975 to 10 November 2000, five rounds of such talks took place under the auspices of the United Nations. Turkish intransigence invariably undermined the UN peace process and obstructed progress.

On 16 January 2002 "direct talks" were launched between President Glafcos Clerides and Turkish Cypriot leader Rauf Denktash. Again, no substantive progress was achieved. In an effort to move the process forward, the UN Secretary General presented, on 11 November, a detailed plan for a comprehensive settlement. The plan was resubmitted twice in revised form on 10 December and on 26 February 2003.

The UN Secretary General asked the leaders of the two communities to a meeting in The Hague on 10 March 2003 for talks. They were also to consider submitting the UN plan to a vote by the people of Cyprus. President Tassos Papadopoulos, who had succeeded Clerides, stated that he would be willing to hold a referendum provided there was a legal framework in place to ensure a workable and durable settlement, and that the security aspects of the plan were resolved between Greece and Turkey. However, the Turkish Cypriot leader, with full backing from Turkey, rejected the plan and refused to submit it to a referendum. The talks collapsed.

To diffuse international criticism, the Turkish side was compelled to partially lift illegal restrictions imposed by the occupation forces since 1974 on the movement of Turkish Cypriots to the free areas controlled by the government of Cyprus and of Greek Cypriots to the areas occupied by Turkey. Since the lifting of these restrictions on 23 April 2003, thousands of Turkish and Greek Cypriots have been crossing over daily from the occupied areas to the free areas and vice versa without any serious incidents.

After the collapse of the meeting at The Hague, efforts for a comprehensive settlement to the Cyprus problem came to a stalemate, and much valuable time was lost. On 4 February 2004,

UN Secretary General Kofi Annan and Cypriot President Tassos Papadopoulos, in front chatting, at The Hague, at the start of the one-day meeting aiming at a settlement of the Cyprus problem, 10 March 2003
Photo: European Press Agency

however, the UN Secretary General called for the resumption of negotiations in New York, and on 13 February it was agreed that the two sides would begin negotiating on the basis of the Secretary General's plan, seeking to agree on changes that fell within the parameters of the plan. In case of a continuing deadlock, even after the involvement of Greece and Turkey in the process, the UN Secretary-General, exercising his discretion, would finalise the text, and the two communities would then vote on the plan in separate, simultaneous referenda. The prospect of the finalisation of the plan by the UN Secretary General, in case the parties failed to reach agreement, proved to be a counter-incentive for substantive negotiations first in Cyprus and subsequently Bürgenstock, Switzerland. In fact, no real negotiations took place. The Secretary General submitted his revised, final plan (Annan V) to the two sides on 31 March 2004.

On 24 April 2004, the people of Cyprus voted on the plan through separate referenda held by the two communities, on the UN Secretary

General's revised proposal for the Comprehensive Settlement of the Cyprus Problem. By a vote of 64.9 percent the Turkish Cypriots approved the plan, but a clear majority of 75.8 percent of Greek Cypriots rejected it. The Greek Cypriots felt that the finalised text, which incorporated many unacceptable demands submitted by Turkey at the last minute, was not a balanced document and did not meet their main concerns regarding security and the functionality and viability of the solution. By their vote, the Greek Cypriots did not reject a solution to the Cyprus problem, which remains their primary goal. They only rejected the particular plan (Annan V) which was placed before them.

For a solution to the Cyprus problem to be viable and to stand the test of time, it must be both fair and perceived as such by the people who will have to live with it. Such a solution, therefore, must be democratic, just, workable, financially viable, and compatible with EU principles, laws and democratic norms, the Convention on Human Rights and key UN resolutions.

Even though that UN effort did not succeed in resolving the Cyprus problem, Greek Cypriots did not believe that it was the end of the road. With this in mind, exploratory talks were held in 2005 with the UN on the possible resumption of the peace process. The agreement between the President of Cyprus and the UN Secretary General in Paris on 28 February 2006 «to continue their ongoing dialogue with the expressed aim at accelerating the search for a comprehensive solution to the Cyprus problem», generated a new momentum for the resumption of the peace process. On 8 July President Tassos Papadopoulos and Turkish Cypriot leader Mehmet Ali Talat held a joint meeting during which they agreed on the following set of principles:

1. Commitment to the unification of Cyprus based on a bi-zonal, bi-communal federation and political equality, as set out in the relevant Security Council resolutions.
2. Recognition of the fact that the status quo is unacceptable and that its prolongation would have negative consequences for the Turkish and Greek Cypriots.
3. Commitment to the proposition that a comprehensive settlement is both desirable and possible, and should not be further delayed.
4. Agreement to begin a process immediately, involving bi-communal discussion of issues that affect the day to day life of the people and concurrently those that concern substantive issues, both of which will contribute to a comprehensive settlement.
5. Commitment to ensure that the 'right atmosphere' prevails for this process to be successful. In that connection, confidence building measures are essential, both in terms of improving the atmosphere and improving the life of all Turkish and Greek Cypriots. Also in that connection, an end must be put to the so-called 'blame game'.

The implementation of the 8 July Agreement, however, is not dependent only on the Greek Cypriot side's good will. It also depends on the stance of the Turkish Cypriot community. Unfortunately, the efforts of the Turkish side for the political upgrading of the illegal secessionist regime, its insistence on the myth of the so-called isolation of the Turkish Cypriot community and the intransigent and provocative statements by Turkish officials, contribute neither to the efforts for the implementation of the 8 July Agreement nor to the goal for a just, mutually acceptable and functional solution to the problem.

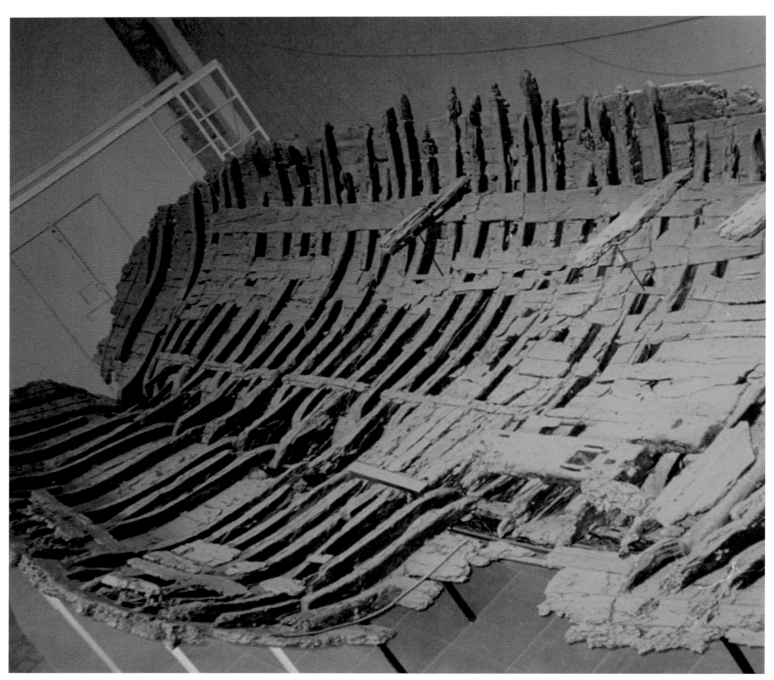

The ancient Keryneia ship as was restored and preserved in the Keryneia castle(*) in 1974

Photo: Press and Information Office

The Keryneia Ship

The Ancient Keryneia Ship

With the cargo in her hull and covered with silt, lying in the depths of the sea with her body gradually dissolving through the centuries, the small ship waited off the coast of Keryneia. She was small but well built; she had sailed all over the Mediterranean Sea until she met her fate on her last voyage.

She sailed to the islands of the Eastern Aegean Sea and picked up olive oil from Samos, wine from Rhodes, millstones, almonds and iron. Then, she set out for Keryneia, Cyprus, with a captain and three sailors. For unknown reasons, the ship sank in the year 300 B.C. Andreas Kariolou, a diver from Keryneia exploring the seabed, was the first to spot the ship in 1965.

Amphorae found in the Keryneia wreck   Photo: Press and Information Office

With permission from the government of Cyprus, a team of archaeologists from the University of Pennsylvania Museum under Professor Michael Katzev raised, preserved and restored the ancient wreck. The underwater operation was conducted with scientific precision. It took eight years (1967-1974) for the restoration to be completed.

With a length of 14.75 metres and a width of 3.4 metres, she could carry a cargo up to 30 tons. Her last cargo consisted of 404 amphorae (dating to the end of the fourth century B.C.), 29 millstones, almonds and iron. A few personal belongings of the crew were also discovered. Some pieces of lead, some tools, some crockery and other items found provide useful information about life on an ancient vessel. The remnants of food—one head of garlic, 18 olive pips, 14 760 fig seeds, about 10 000 almonds whose shells were preserved—paint a vivid picture of the sailors' everyday diet.

After her preservation and restoration, the ship was kept in a special gallery at the Keryneia Castle, where it was studied by scholars and admired by both foreign and local visitors. Unfortunately, the Turkish invasion put a stop to the study of the ancient vessel.

Keryneia II

On 1 November 1982, the Hellenic Institute for the Preservation of Nautical Tradition (H.I.P.N.T.) announced the beginning of a project to replicate in the same dimensions the ancient Keryneia ship. The replication was undertaken by H.I.P.N.T. in collaboration with the Institute of Archaeology of Texas A&M University. The studies carried out before 1974 gave the necessary data toward the replication of the ship. Contemporary ship builders at Manolis Psaros shipyard at Perama, Greece, followed the techniques of the ancient Greeks.

The Keryneia II

Photo: Press and Information Office

The *Keryneia II* was the result of a unique experiment in nautical archaeology. Its main purpose was to attempt to construct the replica by employing the same method as the ancient Greeks had done in building the original, using the "shell first" method (first the keel and planning and then the frames). The materials used in the replica were, as far as possible, comparable to those of the ancient ship.

The *Keryneia II* was finished by June 1985. On 22 June 1985, the new vessel was launched on a long trial sail before attempting to travel to the islands of the Eastern Aegean Sea (Samos, Kos, Nisyros, Rhodes) and Cyprus. Before returning to Cyprus, however, the ship represented Greece in New York during the celebrations of 4-6 July 1986 to honour the centenary of the Statue of Liberty and the anniversary of American Independence. The small vessel received an enthusiastic welcome by the Americans, especially Greek Americans, who saw in her a symbol of Greek harmony and beauty.

Ten persons were trained for the homecoming journey to Cyprus, and Glafkos Kariolou was also invited to join the crew in honour of his father, Andreas Kariolou, the diver who had found the ancient wreck. On 6 September 1986, the vessel sailed from Piraeus and followed the same route which, according to clues and calculations by specialists, was followed by the ancient ship. She stopped at Sounion, then at Kythnos, Syros, Naxos, Kos, Nisyros and Rhodes. She carried the same kind of cargo the ancient vessel had done and whatever was symbolically offered by the islanders. By the end of October 1986, the unpretentious but sailable *Keryneia II* entered the port of Pafos.

As at every other port she had sailed to, so at Pafos she received a warm and proud welcome. For the Cypriots, she was not only a scientific achievement but also a national symbol that represented the hope of returning to Keryneia, a hope never to be lost, and the will to resist and fight till *Keryneia II*, with a Cypriot crew, sails home to her own port, that of Keryneia.

The vessel is now permanently installed in the Ayia Napa Maritime History Museum, in Cyprus.

Keryneia III

The *Keryneia II* took part in the Opening Sail for the 100 years of the Hamburg harbour and in the World Exhibition in Seville. During the Asian Pacific exposition in 1989 it joined the «Silk Road» project of the Japanese state radio and television NHK.

Following the participation of *Keryneia II* in the "Silk Road" project, Yasugi Hamagami, executive producer of NHK, and other admirers of Hellenic History requested permission to construct an exact replica of the Keryneia shipwreck to be permanently exhibited in Japan. Japanese traditional craftsmen constructed the replica, named *Keryneia III*, which has since 1990 been exhibited in a museum in the town of Fukuoka, a permanent ambassador of Cyprus to Japan.

Keryneia-Liberty

The Keryneia – Chrysocava Cultural Foundation, in cooperation with the Keryneia Nautical Club and the municipality of Keryneia, decided in 2002 on the construction of a third replica of the ancient ship of Keryneia to be named *Keryneia-Liberty*.

Since the major objective of *Keryneia-Liberty* was not to duplicate the first and very successful experiment of *Keryneia II*, but rather to continuously experiment with ancient mariner methods and capabilities of sailing, modern fast traditional boat building methods were employed. The project was undertaken by the Avgoustis Brothers Boatyard in Limassol, Cyprus.

The Keryneia - Liberty *on sail*

Photo: Takis Neophytou

The Keryneia - Liberty

On 17 April 2004, the ship left Cyprus for Piraeus and Athens, host city of the Olympic Games. Bringing a message of peace, unity and freedom, the crew delivered to the Mayor of Athens the gifts it was carrying: olive oil from Keryneia, almonds from Nicosia and copper from Cyprus mines to be used for the Olympic Games bronze medals.

The Basilica at Kourion

Outline of the Cyprus Archaeological Heritage

Neolithic Period (c.8300 – c.3900 B.C.)

Chalcolithic-Copper Age (3900 – 2500 B.C.)

Bronze Age (2500 – 1050 B.C.)

Iron Age (1050 B.C. – 330 A.D.)

Byzantine Period (330 – 1191 A.D.)

Frankish - Venetian Period (1191-1571 A.D.)

Part of the Aceramic Neolithic settlement at Khirokitia, c.7000 – 6000 B.C.

Neolithic Period
(c.8300 – c.3900 B.C.)

Located at a privileged position among the Aegean Islands and the coastal areas of Anatolia, Phoenicia, Syria, Palestine and Egypt, Cyprus became one of the most important cultural centres in antiquity and the meeting place of the oldest and greatest Mediterranean civilisations.

The Greek name of the island, *Kypros*, was in the past accompanied by certain characteristic adjectives denoting its natural beauties and resources, like *Dasoessa* for its extensive forests and abundant timber, *Chalcoessa* for its inexhaustible *chalcos* (copper), *Aphrodisia* (Island of Aphrodite), the most popular appellation, for being the birthplace of the goddess.

The earliest specimens of human occupation excavated so far in Cyprus are dated to c.8300 B.C. and fall into the Aceramic Neolithic Period. They consist of a child's skeleton and several adult skulls, discovered together with bones of pig, sheep, goat and deer in two separate wells at Kissonerga – «Mylouthkia». Similar remains of both human and animal bones, including an intact skeleton of the world's earliest domesticated cat and a cat's stone figurine, ascribed to the same period but dating to the eighth and early seventh millennium B.C., were also uncovered at Pareklisia – «Shyllourokambos». However, the general archaeological data of the Cypriot Aceramic Neolithic period are concentrated in the settlements of Khirokitia and Kalavassos – «Tenta», in the free areas of the island, and at «Troulli», «Petra tou Limniti» and Ayios Andreas cape – «Kastros», in the occupied areas (henceforth simply marked with an asterisk) (*).

Andesite spouted bowl from the Aceramic Neolithic settlement of Khirokitia, decorated with parallel chevrons and dotted abstract motifs in relief, c. 6500 B.C., Cyprus Museum

The architectural remains and movable finds produced in these settlements are indicative of well-organised communities with an advanced and well developed standard of living. They also testify that the first known inhabitants of the island, whose place of origin is so far obscure and uncertain, lived in circular private houses, well-built of river stones, rubble and mud-bricks and practiced certain religious rites and burial customs possibly connected with the veneration and cult of the dead. They were also skillful farmers, hunters, fishermen, technicians, potters and jewelers and quite familiar with handicraft, weaving, fanning, navigation and commerce as well.

Farmers mainly dealt with the cultivation of the earth and the production of wheat and grain, beans and peas, lentils, olives and grapes, the domestication of pigs, sheep and goats for their meat, milk, wool and leather. Fishermen and hunters enriched the daily diet with fresh fish and meat of wild pigs, fallow deer, mouflon and various birds.

Necklace of dentalium bead shells and precious stones from the Aceramic Neolithic settlement of Khirokitia, c. 6500 B.C.

Potters and other technicians produced all the necessary agricultural tools and household utensils made entirely of hard river stone, such as plain and decorated andesite vessels, axe-heads, grinders, mortars, querns and pounders. Other technicians, specialists in minor art and jewelry, made bone needles and hooks, flint sickle blades, arrow heads and mace heads, crude idols and remarkable necklaces and pendants of dentalium shell beads, cornelian, hematite and other precious stones, imported together with obsidian blades from Syria and Anatolia in exchange for various Cypriot products.

By the end of the seventh millennium B.C., the Aceramic Neolithic Period was followed by the destruction and abandonment of the first settlements, accompanied by withering and general decay, which continued for about 1 500 years. In c.4500 B.C., that dark period of miseries and disasters was succeeded by the Ceramic Neolithic Period, which lasted until c.3900 B.C. This is represented by the settlements of Sotira – «Teppes», Kalavassos A, the upper layers of the Khirokitia site, Ayios Epiktitos – «Vrysi» (*) and Philia – Drakos (*). From the beginning of that second phase of the Cypriot Neolithic era, not only stone, but also clay was in use for the manufacture of vessels and household utensils. The clay vases uncovered in the excavated settlements comprise various plain and decorated water jugs of

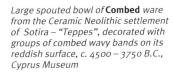

*Large spouted bowl of **Combed** ware from the Ceramic Neolithic settlement of Sotira – "Teppes", decorated with groups of combed wavy bands on its reddish surface, c. 4500 – 3750 B.C., Cyprus Museum*

Red Lustrous and Red on White wares, but mostly large spouted milk bowls of Combed ware with a unique combed linear decoration. That innovation in pottery, combined with the parallel production of elaborate stone vessels, implements and ornaments in large quantities, indicates a high level of economic, social and cultural development.

Chalcolithic-Copper Age
(3900 – 2500 B.C.)

Like the Neolithic Age, the next period, the Chalcolithic – Copper Age, is divided into two successive periods, the Chalcolithic I and Chalcolithic II, dating to 3900-2900 B.C. and to 2900-2500 B.C., respectively. The first period is represented by the settlements of Erimi – Pambula, Kalavassos – «Kopetra» and both the settlement and cemetery of Souskiou – «Vathyrkakas», the second period by similar sites revealed at Lemba – «Lakkous», Kissonerga – «Mosphilia» and «Milouthkia», Philia – «Drakos»(*) and Ambelikou – «Ayios Georgios» (*).

Thanks to the discovery and smelting of copper and the development of commerce, a robust economy and general progress were created and stabilised during the entire Chalcolithic era. The architectural remains unearthed attest that, parallel to the continuation of the previously stone-built circular houses, new wooden rectangular houses, dressed with thick layers of clay and provided with stone hearths on their earthen floors, were constructed. In addition, the Chalcolithic cemetery of Souskiou – «Vathyrkakas» which is completely separated from its nearby settlement suggests that, except for the preservation of the Neolithic custom mentioned above, the dead were also buried in proper rock-cut, pit-shaped tombs grouped next to each other in independent cemeteries.

Besides, the uncovered tomb gifts and many other similar finds from the excavated settlements include the first specimens of copper objects, a chisel and a hook from Erimi, a spiral ornament from Souskiou – «Vathyrkakas» and similar items from the Kissonerga settlements which confirm the addition of copper to stone and clay for the production of handicraft objects and justify the name Chalcolithic given to that period. They also include large

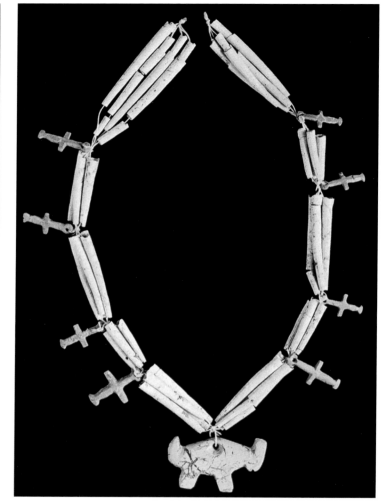

Necklace of dentalium bead shells and miniature picrolite cruciform figurines with a central animal-shaped pendant from the Souskiou – «Vathyrkakas» Chalcolithic I cemetery, c. 3000 B.C., Cyprus Museum

Clay bowl with three long feet of the developed **Red-on-White** *ware from the Chalcolithic II settlement of Ambelikou – "Ayios Georghios"(*) decorated with linear geometric designs on its whitish surface, c. 2700 B.C., Cyprus Museum*

storage pots, handleless bowls, jugs, bird-shaped and animal-shaped askoi, composite ritual and monster shaped vases, lentoid flasks and bottles with pointed bases of the new Monochrome ware and the developed White Painted ware. Among the gifts were also various tiny bone and stone pendants and figurines, exceptional ladies' ornaments, mainly necklaces and pendants, but especially large picrolite figurines either in the form of naked women with accentuated incised breasts or in the shape of cruciform, depicting a stylised complex of two joint figures, a male and a female, which were considered as the symbolic cult objects of the fertility goddess. A large deep bowl from Kissonerga – «Mosphilia», found full of terracotta figurines mixed with several small stone objects and interpreted as a model of an open-air, circular sanctuary, testifies to the development of a deeply religious sentiment and the beginning of the cult of the fertility goddess in certain sanctuaries from the Middle Chalcolithic Period.

Picrolite cruciform figurine of the Chaloclithic I Period from Pafos, bearing a necklace with a pendant in the form of a similar figurine, c. 3500 B.C., Cyprus Museum

Bronze Age
(2500 – 1050 B.C.)

The Chalcolithic era was succeeded by the Bronze Age, which is divided into the Early, Middle and Late Bronze Age, dating to 2500-1900 B.C., 1900-1650 and 1650-1050 B.C., respectively. The Early Bronze Age is represented by the settlements at Kyra – Alonia(*), Sotira – «Kaminouthkia», Margi – «Alonia» and the cemeteries at Pellapais – «Vounous» (*), Dhenia (*), Lapithos (*), Kotsiatis, Avdimou, Ayia Paraskevi – Nicosia, and others. The Middle Bronze Age is illustrated by the settlements of Kalopsida (*), Episkopi – «Pambula» and Alambra – «Mouttes» and the Late Bronze Age in the sites of Enkomi, Kition, «Hala-Sultan Tekke», Kalavassos – Ayios Dimitrios, Pyla – «Kokkinokremmos», Alassa, Palaepafos and Maa – Palaeokastro.

The three stages of the Bronze Age are characterised by continuous commercial, social and cultural progress accompanied by wealth and prosperity that reached their peak during the Cypro-Mycenaean

Clay model of an open-air circular sanctuary of the Early Bronze Age from Pellapais – "Vounous"(*) enclosing groups of human figures, participating in a certain ceremony, and bulls' led for sacrifice in honour of the divinities depicted in relief against the wall of the sanctuary, holding snakes and wearing bulls' masks, the symbols of the Fertility goddess and the Death divinity, c. 2500-2300 B.C., Cyprus Museum

Period (c.1450-1050 B.C.). This is entirely due to the abundant production and export to neighbouring Greece and Egypt of Cypriot copper together with pottery and other objects in exchange for gold, silver, tin, alabaster, faience and precious stones. The first striking innovations appear on the remarkable Early Bronze Age clay vessels of the new Red Polished ware, consisting of various human and animal-shaped vases, stemmed and spouted bowls, ovoid jugs with cut-away necks and boat-shaped pyxises with incised and relief decoration of bullheads, snakes, deer and human figures holding infants and obviously representing the fertility goddess, whose worship was definitely continuing in a more intense way. This fact is indicated by various other exceptional Red Polished pottery items from Vounous, including several composite ritual jugs and a unique clay model of a sanctuary.

*Early Bronze Age composite ritual vase of **Red Polished** ware from Pellapais – "Vounous" (*) consisting of one main jug with a long cylindrical neck and seven smaller jugs, attached and communicating to each other, c.200-2000 B.C., Cyprus Museum*

The rest of the Early Bronze Age developed types of pottery, metallurgy and minor art which replaced and displaced all the earlier stone objects, and which are represented by other clay models of sanctuaries, planked-shaped female figurines holding infants, bronze sickle and knife blades, swords, daggers, axes, chisels, hair locks, earrings, bracelets, rings and the first gold earring from Sotira – «Kaminouthhkia».

Other innovations are distinctive of tomb architecture and burial customs: The pit-shaped tombs of the previous period were replaced by new rock-cut tombs, which consisted of a *dromos* (vertical passage), a cave-shaped chamber in which the dead were buried together with various offerings, and a *stomion* (entrance), which was closed by a large limestone slab or blocked with rough stones and peddles after the burial.

The same religious beliefs, burial customs and works of metallurgy and minor art continued in the Middle Bronze Age parallel to the obvious development of tomb architecture and some other sectors of art. Particularly, some of the rock-cut tombs were covered by earthen tumuli after the burial, a new custom from Syria and Palestine.On the south side of the chamber of a tomb at Karmi – Palialona(*) a human figure was carved, the first tomb sculpture in Prehistoric Cyprus. Besides, the architectural remains of a fortress at Nitovikla (*) of Karpassia and other similar ruins at «Krini»(*) – Keryneia, Dhikomo(*), «Nicolaides» – Nicosia and Ayios Sozomenos indicate the development of military architecture probably connected with the Hyksos raids on the island. The pottery also is represented by the new White Painted and Black on Red wares, which replaced the earlier Red Polished

Early Bronze Age pyxises of the **Red Polished** *ware from Pellapais – "Vounous"(*), decorated with groups of incised zig-zag and parallel lines and opposite standing male and female figures holding infants, clear symbols of the Fertility goddess, c. 2500 – 2300 B.C., Cyprus Museum*

Middle Bronze Age jug of **White Painted** *ware from a tomb at Lapithos(*), with cut away neck, standing figures on shoulder and elegant rich, linear, decoration in black paint all over its surface, c. 1750 B.C., Cyprus Museum*

Partial view of the architectural remains of Enkomi (*), including the sanctuaries of the **Horned God** *and* **Ingot God***, c. 1200 B.C.*

The sanctuary of Aphrodite at Palaepafos, c. 1200 B.C.

ware and appeared with large quantities of bowls, jugs, *askoi* and human, animal and bird-shaped vases decorated with linear and other geometric motifs on their white and black surfaces.

The Late Bronze Age constitutes the most important and prosperous stage of the entire Prehistoric era of Cyprus. This is exclusively due to the uninterrupted commercial and cultural links of the island with all its neighbouring countries, but especially to its closer contacts with the Aegean region and Crete. These contacts were intensified and reached their peak during the Cypro-Mycenaean Period (c.1400-1050 B.C.). The first Mycenaeans-Achaeans started to come in Cyprus in c.1400 B.C. as traders and craftsmen, using the major harbour towns as their stations and commercial centres. By the end of the thirteenth century B.C., a wave of colonists established themselves permanently in various places, and later, at the end of the twelfth century, a second wave arrived on the island introducing, along with their language, religion, customs and traditions, innovations in all the sectors of art and the legislation of kingdoms as well. The island was fully

Single and composite jugs of **Base-Ring** *ware, decorated with bands and spirals in relief and imitating metallic prototypes, c. 1650 -1500 B.C., Cyprus Museum*

hellenised. However, the first elements of the island's Greek cultural heritage appeared much earlier and obviously were introduced directly from Crete in c.1500 B.C. They are incised on a rectangular clay tablet from Enkomi and constitute the earliest specimens of the

Cypriot script, the so-called Cypro-Minoan script, which is similar to the undeciphered Creto-Minoan Linear A script, and which was in use at least until the end of the Late Bronze Age. It was succeeded by the Cypro-Syllabic script, which consisted of 55 linear signs and was deciphered by George Smith in 1876. Resembling the Mycenaean Linear B script, which was deciphered by Michael Ventris in 1952, the Cypro-Syllabic script was continued, parallel to the Greek Alphabet, until the early Hellenistic Period.

The intense Mycenaean influence appears in architecture, town planning and religion and is clearly reflected on the ruins of imposing public ashlar buildings and ordinary houses in well-organised towns, like Enkomi and Kition, both of which were fortified by cyclopean walls, imitating the monumental defensive prototypes of Mycenae, Tyrins and other contemporary sites in Greece. The new public buildings include the two sanctuaries excavated at Enkomi and dedicated to the Horned God, identified with Apollo Kereates – protector god of cattle and patron of shepherds, in Arcadia of the Peloponnese, and Ingot God – protector of the Cypriot copper mines. They also include the sanctuary of Aphrodite at Palaepafos, a group of four temples at Kition – «Kathari» and the public buildings of administrative character at Alassa and Kalavassos – «Ayios Dimitrios», all dating to the beginning of the twelfth century B.C.

The same Mycenaean influence is demonstrated in tomb architecture and burial

Bowls of **White Slip** *ware with wish-bone handles and geometric linear decoration in mat black paint, c. 1600 – 1450 B.C.*

Conical rhyton of faience from Kition, separated in three zones filled with representations of galloping animals, bull hunting and running spirals, c. 1300 B.C., Cyprus Museum

Cypro -Mycenaean amphoroid craters of Pictorial style from Enkomi, decorated, one with octopuses and chariots drawn by horses on both sides, c. 1400 B.C., Cyprus Museum

customs, presenting new rock-cut chambered tombs with short sloping *dromoi* in various cemeteries and the earliest built tombs with flat roofs and *tholoi* furnished with rich offerings. It is also expressed even stronger on pottery, metallurgy and minor art. The pottery of the first phase of the Late Bronze Age consists mostly of jugs of the Monochrome and Base Ring wares, covered with brownish slip and decorated with bands and spirals in relief, jugs and bowls of White Slip Ware, decorated with geometric motifs and jug lets of White Shaved ware with pointed bases.

Cypro-Mycenaean pottery is represented by a large variety of outstanding specimens of vessels including amphoroid, bell-shaped and open large craters, bowls caps, *skyphoi*, flasks, *rhyta* and stirrup jars of the Pictorial style, Pastoral or Rude Style, Granary style and the sub-Mycenaean Proto-White Painted ware made of clay, faience, silver and alabaster and decorated with human and animal figures, mythological scenes, chariots, octopuses, birds and various floral motifs.

*Bronze stand from Kourion with four legs, supporting a ring, and decoration of four human figures in panels in front of the **"sacred tree"**, three standing and carrying fish and a bronze ingot on their shoulders and one seated and playing her lyre, c. 1200 B.C., British Museum, London*

Metallurgy and minor art, apart from weapons, implements and household utensils, which continued the previous tradition in more developed types, present numerous incomparable ornaments, made of gold and silver and including necklaces with gold beads in the forms of eight-shaped shields, dates and pomegranates, in some cases alternated with precious stones, bracelets with wrapped endings, circular earrings with hanged bull's heads, and cylindrical finger-rings with bezels of incised animal figures. They also present bronze stands decorated with human figures in various postures and the first two bronze statuettes representing the Horned God and the Ingot God, both from Enkomi.

In addition to the fantastic gold, silver and bronze ornaments, many other spectacular items of minor art, made of imported precious stones and ivory, were produced in abundance comprising various conoid stamp seals and scarabs with incised human figures, deities, heroes, bulls, sacred trees and ivory mirror handles, pipes, draught-boxes and other objects discovered with pictorial compositions in relief and incised patterns.

Necklace from Ayios Iakovos (*) with gold beads, in the forms of dates and pomegranates, and pendant of an engraved lapis lazuli cylinder seal, c. 1300 B.C., Cyprus Museum

Ivory mirror handle from a tomb at Palaepafos, with decoration of incised patterns and a composition of a warrior in relief, stabbing a lion with a dagger and resembling the mythological scene of Heracles killing the Nemean Lion, c. 1200 B.C., Cyprus Museum

Silver bowl from Enkomi (*), with embossed decoration of bull's heads, rosettes and lotus flowers in gold and niello, c. 1400-1350 B.C., Cyprus Museum

*Bronze statuette of the **Ingot God**, the god protector of the Cypriot copper mines, from his sanctuary at Enkomi (*), standing on a copper ingot and armed with a horned helmet, shield and spear, c. 1200 B.C., Cyprus Museum*

Iron Age
(1050 B.C.– 330 A.D.)

The Iron Age is divided into the Geometric Period (1050-750 B.C.), the Archaic Period (725-475 B.C.), the Classical period (475-325 B.C.), the Hellenistic Period (325-50 B.C.) and the Roman Period (50 B.C.-330 A.D.).

Excluding the Roman Period, remains of public buildings and private houses from all the other periods are very limited and restricted to the ruins of the following structures: the Phoenician temple of Astarte at Kition and the non-existent sanctuaries at Ayios Iakovos (*) and Idalion of the Geometric Period; the private houses at Salamis (*), Kition and Tamassos of the Archaic Period and the non-existent sanctuaries at Meniko and Ayia Irini (*), the sanctuary at Polis and the Phoenician sanctuary of Heracles Melkaart at Kition of the same period; the palace and temple of Athina at Soli – Vouni(*), the pyramidal glacis at Kourion and the public building at Palaepafos-Hadjiabtoullah of the Classical Period; the theatre at Pafos and private houses at Kourion, Kition, Amathus, Salamis(*), and Soli(*) and the non-existing temples of Aphrodite, Kybeli, Isis and Serapis at Soli-Hollades of the Hellenistic Period.

In contrast, the Roman Period is represented by numerous architectural remains of public buildings and patrician and ordinary private houses: the theatres of Salamis (*), Kourion and Soli (*), the gymnasia, public baths and *stadia* of Salamis (*), and Kourion, *agorae-fora* of Salamis(*), Amathus, Kourion, Pafos and Soli (*), the temples of Zeus at Salamis (*), Apollo Hylates at Kourion and Aphrodite at Amathus, the Odeion at Pafos, the Nymphaea at Kourion and Soli(*) and the Patrician Houses of Gladiators and Achilles at Kourion and Dionysos, Theseus, Aion and Orpheus at Pafos, the floors of which are paved with multicoloured mosaic compositions of mythological scenes, hunting scenes, paradise birds framed by a large variety of intricate geometric designs and floral motifs. In 1980 the invaluable mosaic wealth and all the other monuments of Nea Pafos together with the outstanding sanctuary of Aphrodite at Palaepafos were honoured by UNESCO and were included on the World's Heritage List.

Tomb architecture and burial customs, pottery and generally all other sectors of art appear with sufficient and concrete evidence of distinct

The theatre of Soli (*), constructed in the early second century A.D. , destroyed and abandoned in the mid fourth century A.D. and reconstructed in 1962 by the Cyprus Department of Antiquities

The gymnasium of Salamis(*), dating to the first century A.D. and consisting of an open rectangular palaestra (place for wrestling) surrounded by four colonnaded porticoes and a large complex of baths, joined with the east portico

The Palace of Vouni(*), consisting of the royal rooms, baths, store-rooms and water tanks. Originally it was constructed in Anatolian style, probably by the pro-Persian king of Marion Stasiikos to watch and control the anti-Persian movements of the pro-Greek Solians, but in the mid fifth century it was modified in a clear Greek style, resembling the Mycenaean Megaron, 500-380 B.C.

innovations and development. During the Geometric Period tomb architecture continued the earlier tradition of rock-cut chambered tombs but, in addition to the custom of the usual inhumations, the first cremations and burials of slaves together with their masters took place in some tombs at Lapithos(*) and Kourion-«Kaloriziki», respectively.

The public baths of Kourion, dating to the first century A.D. and consisting of two units of **"Thermae"** *– hot baths, separated by a central open courtyard and the* **Nymphaeum** *of Kourion*

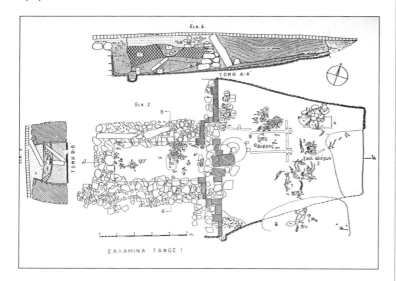

Plan of the **"Royal" Tomb** *1 at Salamis (*), showing burials of chariots and horses in its dromos and human skeleton remains together with dead offerings in its chamber*

By the beginning of the Archaic Period, parallel to the rock-cut tombs, new huge subterranean tombs, comprising long and wide sloping *dromoi* and rectangular chambers with flat, curved and triangular roofs started to be constructed with well-hewn limestone blocks and continued their existence until the end of the fourth century B.C. Some of these tombs had two chambers on the same axis and other side-chambers, while others were covered with tumuli. Nine of them were excavated at Salamis (*), ten at Amathus, two at Kition, two at Tamassos, two at Patriki, two at Xylotymbou, one at Trahonas (*), one

Mosaic composition on the floor of a room in the House of Dionysos at Pafos, representing the triumphant procession of Dionysos after his successful military expedition to India

furniture dressed with ivory, recalling the throne of Penelope and the bed of Odysseus and imitating in general Homeric burial customs.

During the Hellenistic Period, the Archaic and Classical built royal tombs were replaced by other huge monumental but rock-cut tombs. These tombs, parallel to the use of cenotaphs and small rock-cut chambered tombs with stepped *dromoi*, continued their tradition in the Roman period.

Pottery, which was entirely wheel-made, presents very developed vessels in the shapes of amphorae, bowls, dishes, kylixes, craters, *dinoi*, jugs, kernoi, *askoi* and goblets of the new Black Slip-Buccero, White Painted, Bichrome, Black-on-Red and Plain White wares, decorated with various geometric designs during the entire Geometric Period and pictorial compositions of human and animal figures at the end of the period. Most of those types continued in the Archaic Period, during which the vase painting demonstrates a skillful combination of geometric designs with lotus flowers, palm trees, rosettes, sphinxes and stylised bulls, birds and fish in the new Free Field style ware, indicating strong Near Eastern and Egyptian influences.

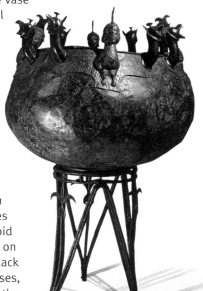

Bronze cauldron supported on an iron tripod from the "Royal" Tomb 79 at Salamis (*), with decoration of eight griffin protomes and four double-faced sirens on its rim

In the Cypro-Classical Period, apart from the previous White Painted, Bichrome and Plain White wares, new types of vases appear including large ovoid spouted jugs with plastic figure on their shoulders, the famous Black Figured and Red Figured Attic Vases, the Rhodian «Fikellura» and the Corinthian and Euboian types in the shapes of amphora, jug, lekythos, kylix, *askos*, aryballos, alabastron, dish, bowl e.t.c., decorated with Greek mythological scenes combined with floral and geometric designs.

at Pyla and one at Kourion. Although the chambers of the tombs were all looted, most of their *dromoi*, especially those of the Salamis royal tombs yielded numerous selected offerings, including chariots and skeletons of sacrificed horses and slaves to serve their masters in the afterlife, bronze cauldrons, amphorae filled with olive oil and wooden

Wooden bed from the **"Royal" Tomb** *79 at Salamis (*), inlaid with ivory and dated to the end of the eighth century B.C.*

One of the **"Tombs of the Kings"** *in Pafos, dating to the Early Hellenistic Period and consisting of an open rectangular, peristyle courtyard with limestone columns in the Doric style*

*Amphora of the Cypro-***Geometric White Painted** *ware, decorated with bands, parallel and zig-zag lines and solid black paint on rim, c. 950-850 B.C., Cyprus Museum*

*Jug of the Cypro-***Archaic Free-Field** *style, with pinched rim and decorated with stylised bird and fish in bichrome black and red paint*

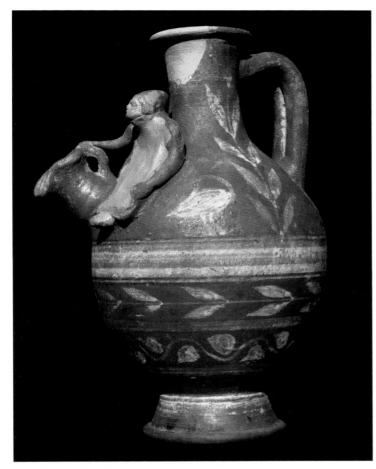

*Cypro-**Classical** jug with a long cylindrical neck, small spout and tiny plastic female figure pouring water from a juglette, c. 475 – 450 B.C., Cyprus Museum*

Apart from clay vases, Iron Age ceramics include various figurines, oil lamps and other objects of minor art. Geometric and Archaic figurines are almost similar and comprise compact cylindrical and hollow bell-shaped warriors, musicians, horse riders, horse-drawn chariots, scenes of daily life including childbirth, etc. The classical figurines represent mostly *korae*, imitating the corresponding Greek Tanagra Korae, while the Hellenistic and Roman depict mainly human figures and deities, among them Eros in various postures, satyrs, the Rape of Ganymedes by Zeus, Hermes Kourotrophos and especially nude Aphrodite, indicating that the goddess continued to be worshiped together with Zeus, Apollo Hylates, Athena, Hermes, and with other Greek Olympian gods in their sanctuaries until the end of the Iron Age.

*Cypro-**Classical Black-Figured** jug decorated with human figures in black paint on red slip, c. 475-450 B.C., Cyprus Museum*

During the Hellenistic Period, most of the previous types were replaced by the new Black Glazed and Red Glazed wares and various vases made of light green-blue or honey-colour glass. The shapes of the vases included small ehinoi (handleless bowls), bottles, skyphoi, unguentaria (perfume pots) of both the new types, amphorae with pointed bases, *skyphoi* and lagynoi of the previous developed Plain White and White Painted wares and perfume pots, tear pots, beakers and goblets made of glass, most of which continued to be used in the Roman Period, together with the new Terra Sigillata clay stamped vases which replaced most of the previous Hellenistic types.

The first specimens of oil lamps appeared in the Early Archaic Period in the saucer-shaped type, with claw feet and decoration of abstract designs in relief or bands in red and black paint. They continued in the Classical Period in similar types, but with pinched and rounded rim, higher foot and floral decoration in relief, and even in the Hellenistic Period, but covered with black or red shiny paint. During the Roman Period most of them followed the Terra Sigillata pottery type with moulten designs in relief, while some were decorated with human and animal figures, erotic scenes and other compositions including a head of Medusa, Zeus seated on a throne, Heracles killing Lernea Hydra, etc.

*Terracotta figurines of the Cypro-**Archaic Period**, representing a group of five musicians and a horse with a rider, c. 650 B.C., Cyprus Museum*

*Limestone statue of a Kouros (youth) with the characteristic **Archaic** smile and projection of the left foot, similar to the corresponding **Archaic** prototypes on mainland Greece, c. 650 B.C., Cyprus Museum*

Hellenistic lagynos with biconical depressed body, vertical rope-shaped handle and decoration of geometric linear designs and floral motifs, c.300 -250 B.C., Cyprus Museum

Limestone funerary votive stele from Marion depicting a seated woman holding a bird in her left arm, whose name is engraved in the Cypro-syllabic script behind her head and reads: "I am Aristila from Salamis, daughter of Onasis"

The earliest samples of Cypriot plastic art and sculpture fall into the mid-seventh century B.C. and consist of various small-size, life-size and over-size statues of limestone and clay with mainly flattened bodies and conical cover on head suggesting strong influence from the Near East. In the sixth century, they appear with an obvious influence from Egypt and present faces with large almond-shaped eyes, symmetrical noses and thin lips. By the beginning of the fifth century B.C., the Cypro-Ionian types of *kouroi* and *korae* with an elaborate dress of chiton and himation, thin facial characteristics and rich decoration on heads dominate on the Cypriot sculpture.

During the Cypro-Classical Period, sculpture works in general demonstrate a rapid development with intense Greek influence and display spectacular specimens of statues and funerary votive stelae of limestone, marble and bronze with idealised and realistic facial characteristics and body details. They continued their artistic perfection in the entire Hellenistic period, inspired by the corresponding masterpieces of Greek Classical sculpture.

In the entire Roman Period, sculpture works were produced with the same materials but in larger quantities, comprising statues and portraits of deities, heroes, emperors, athletes, etc., with accentuated, natural and symmetrical facial characteristics mostly influenced by sculpture works of the Greco-Roman centres of Alexandria and Cyrene.

Strengthened by the new material of iron in the middle of the eleventh century B.C., the metallurgy of the Iron Age is characterised by an intensive and continuous rhythm of development. It presents larger quantities and better qualities of metal work, including harder and stronger sickle blades, axes, knife blades and daggers made of iron. However, the rest of its products are mostly represented by numerous impressive large bowls, skewers, tripods and swords made of copper and bronze found in various Geometric and Archaic tombs, especially at Salamis and Pafos-Skales.

The objects of minor art, except for the ornaments, continue the tradition of the previous types and include pins, toggle pins, hair locks, bucklets, seals and other tiny items made of iron, copper, bronze, ivory and precious stones. The seals had mainly conical, hemispherical and rectangular shapes and depicted human figures, *bucrania*, deer and goats, on which influences from Greece and the Near East are obvious.

Ornaments include gold, gold-plated, silver and bronze necklaces with golden beads, sometimes alternated with precious stones, pendants in the shape of lotus flowers, boat-shaped earrings and animal-shaped bracelets with ends in figures of goats and bulls, finger rings with engraved precious stones representing deities and other figures, bucklets, gold wreaths of myrtle leaves, etc.

The first silver coins of Evelthon, King of Salamis (575-560 B.C.), depicting his emblem, the ram on the obverse, and the *ank*, the Egyptian symbol of life and good luck, on the reverse, and all the other coins of the later kings of Cyprus, together with bronze oil-lamps, golden and bronze figurines and other objects complete the overall picture of the Iron Age minor art.

Marble head of Aphrodite or Hygeia from the gymnasium of Salamis (*) with idealised facial characteristics, c. 400 B.C., Cyprus Museum

Bronze statuette of a cow from the treasure room of Athena's temple at Vouni (*) with realistic details of body, resembling the corresponding contemporary prototype by the famous Greek sculptor Myron, c. 450 B.C., Cyprus Museum

Limestone head of a young woman from Arsos (*) with symmetrical facial characteristics, recalling the corresponding works of the great Greek sculptor Myron, c. 300 B.C., Cyprus Museum

Marble statue of Aphrodite from Soli (*), whose arms and feet are missing. The rest facial characteristics and body details resemble similar statues from Cyrene, c.100 – 50 B.C., Cyprus Museum

The Early Christian Basilica on the beach at Kourion, consisting of a three - aisled nave with 12 marble columns, eleven of which have been reconstructed, a sanctuary with three apses, a narthex and an atrium with central well, c. 525

Byzantine Period
(330 – 1191 A.D.)

During the Byzantine Period (330-1191 A.D.), Cyprus participated in the Byzantine civilisation spread through Southern and Eastern Europe, with Early Christian Basilicas, represented by those at Soli(*), Salamis(*), Amathus, Kourion, Marion, Peyeia, and Rizokarpasso(*), dating between the fourth and sixth century A.D. They were succeeded by the Byzantine Churches of Panayia Kanakaria at Lythrankomi and Panayia Angeloktisti at Kiti with their famous sixth-century mosaic compositions, Christ Antiphonites at Kalogrea and many other Byzantine and post-Byzantine churches with fantastic specimens of wall paintings.

In 1985, nine of these churches, in the Troodos region, namely Ayios Nicolaos tis Steyis at Kakopetria (eleventh century), Ayios Ioannis Lampadistis at Kalopanayiotis (eleventh century), Panayia Phorviotissa at Asinou (twelfth century), Panayia tou Araka at Lagoudera (twelfth century), Panayia at Moutoulla (thirteenth century), Archangelos at Pedoulas (fifteenth century), Timios Stavros at Pelendri (thirteenth century), Panayia Podhithou at Galata (fifteenth century) and Stavros tou Ayiasmati of Platanistasa (fifteenth century) were included by UNESCO in the World Heritage List, like the sites of Palaepafos and Nea Pafos, in 1980, for their exceptional wall paintings. The earliest of these paintings, those of the eleventh and twelfth centuries, constitute the best masterpieces of Cyprus Byzantine art and are considered as the predecessors of Renaissance art.

Mosaic composition of the Virgin between Archangels Michael and Gabriel, on the sanctuary's apse of the Church of Panayia Angeloktisti, at Kiti, sixth century

The Church of Panayia Podhithou at Galata, fifteenth century

The spacious single-aisled Church of Christ Antiphonitis at Kalogrea(*), decorated with impressive frescoes, including the Baptism of Christ, Archangel Gabriel, several saints and other holy figures, late twelfth century

Fresco of the Dormition of Virgin in the **"Asinou"** Church of Panayia Forviotissa at Nikitari, painted in 1106

Frankish-Venetian Period
(Twelfth-Sixteenth Centuries)

Between the twelfth and sixteenth century, under Lusignan and Venetian rule, Cyprus, influenced by Byzantine art and the art of Medieval Europe, created monumental Frankish castles, Gothic churches and defensive walls, represented by the castles of Keryneia (*), Ayios Ilarion (*), Voufavento (*), Kantara (*), Limassol, Kolossi and Pafos; the Churches of Ayia Sophia (*) in Nicosia and Ayios Nicolaos in Famagusta (*); the Abbey of Pellapais in Keryneia (*); and the defensive walls of Nicosia and Famagusta (*).

Also noteworthy is the island's traditional folk art and architecture, created between the seventeenth and nineteenth centuries and represented by lots of agricultural tools, household utensils and many selected traditional houses, of which the most important have been declared ancient monuments by the Cyprus Department of Antiquities.

The west side of the Gothic abbey at Pellapais(*), Keryneia

The Medieval castle of
Keryneia(*) originally
constructed in the late
ninth century but
remodeled and extended
in the late thirteenth
century

The Church of Ayios Nicolaos, Famagusta (*), now a mosque

The House of Katsinioros at the village of Fikardou, one of the earliest but well preserved Houses of Folk Architecture

The second gallery of the Kykkos Monastery Museum, with objects of the Byzantine and post-Byzantine world
Photo: Perdikis K. Stylianos, Guide to the Museum of the Holy Monastery of Kykkos, Lefkosia 1998

Kykkos Monastery Museum

Tradition has it that Byzantine Emperor Alexios Comnenos I (1081-1118) was prompted to establish the Holy Royal and Stavropegial Monastery of the Virgin of Kykkos. He was so prompted after the hermit Isaiah, who lived in the Troodos Mountains, revealed that the emperor's daughter could be healed from a rare incurable disease, if he would consent to build a monastery and donate to it the icon of the Virgin which he possessed and which, reputedly, was painted by the Apostle Luke.

The fame of the Holy Icon as miracle-working spread throughout Orthodoxy. During the last nine hundred years, thousands of pilgrims, emperors to paupers, have traveled to the monastery to seek the Virgin's help, many of them bearing votive gifts and precious offerings. They would place them before the Virgin's icon as a fulfillment of a vow or in gratitude for a miraculous response to their prayers.

The museum of the monastery was conceived by Abbot Nikiforos. Its purpose was twofold: to reflect the magnificence and majesty of the Byzantine Empire; and to highlight the term "royal," which

The third gallery of the Kykkos Monastery Museum, with icons, frescoes and church furniture
Photo: Perdikis K. Stylianos, Guide to the Museum of the Holy Monastery of Kykkos, Lefkosia 1998

Wood carved cross on a base, probably a work by Georgios Laskaris, 1545 (43,5 H x 10,5 cm)

is part of the official title of the monastery and which binds it directly to the imperial palace of Constantinople, from whence the monastery derived its foundation and endowment. The floors of the museum are made of multi-coloured granite and marble, while the ceilings are covered with walnut and enriched with woodcarving and gilding. The decorative effect is enhanced by iconic and symbolic themes in marble, and by stone carvings and frescoes.

It is also one of the most up-to-date museums on the island, utilising all the latest lighting and climatic devices for the display and preservation of the priceless treasures. Designed to form an integral part of the existing monastery complex, the museum consists of five adjoining areas, four galleries and a gift shop.

The first gallery houses a display of ancient pottery and ceramics, covering a period of twenty-six centuries, from 2300 B.C. – 330 A.D. The second exhibits various objects of the Byzantine and post-Byzantine world, from early Christian times (fourth century A.D.) to the middle of the twentieth century.

The third, an octagonal gallery, has a dome with Christ Pantocrator painted by Sozos Giannoudis. It contains icons, Byzantine frescoes, wood carvings and church furniture.

The fourth, a smaller octagon with built-in showcases, displays documents, gospels, illuminated manuscripts and books published by the monastery.

The museum offers for sale copies of some of the exhibits, photos, and other souvenirs, as well as a guide to the museum authored by its curator, Stylianos K. Perdikis.

Photo: Cyprus Tourism Organisation

Nature and People

The Island

Population

Towns

Climate

Vegetation and Flora

Fauna

The Island

Two mountain ranges run from east to west across the island, separated by the central Messaoria plain.

The densely forested Troodos Range in the southwest is a dome-shaped highland dominated by the island's highest peak, Mount Olympus, at 1 953 metres above sea level. The entire Troodos massif takes up approximately one half the area of the island and constitutes the largest volume of ophiolite rock in the world.

The narrower Keryneia Range in the north is mainly of limestone. Known also as the Pentadaktylos (Five-Finger mountain), it rises up to 1 024 metres.

Cyprus is almost surrounded by coastal valleys where the soil is suitable for agriculture. Arable land constitutes 46.8 percent of the total area of the island. There are no rivers, only torrents which flow after heavy rain.

Avakas gorge in the Akamas peninsula. **Photo: Christos Violaris**

Population

At the end of 2005, the total population of Cyprus was 854 300. Of this, 76.8 percent (656 200) are considered to be members of the Christian Greek Cypriot community and speak Greek. Of the remainder, 10.3 percent (87 900) belong to the Muslim Turkish Cypriot community and speak Turkish, and 12.9 percent (110 200) are foreign workers and expatriates residing in Cyprus. English is widely spoken on the island and regularly used in commerce and government.

While the majority of the Greek Cypriot community are members of the Greek Cypriot Orthodox Church of Cyprus, 1 percent are actually members of the Armenian, Maronite and Latin Churches. Under the provisions of the 1960 Constitution, these small religious communities chose to be considered members of the Greek Cypriot community.

Since the Turkish invasion and occupation of over one third of the island, however, the demographic character has been changed dramatically as a result of Turkey's population policies.

Towns

Nicosia

The capital of Cyprus is Nicosia, with a population of around 224 500. Situated roughly in the middle of the island, it has the unwelcome distinction of being the only divided capital city in the world. Since the Turkish invasion of 1974, its northern part is under occupation and separated from the south by a UN-patrolled buffer zone.

Nicosia is a sprawling cosmopolitan city as well as a commercial centre. The old city is quaint, surrounded by Venetian Walls built in

the sixteenth century, with narrow streets, sidewalk tavernas, restored buildings and tourist shops that bring history to life.

Limassol

The second largest town is Limasol, the main commercial port of Cyprus. With a population of around 176 900, it is also a popular tourist resort and a major business centre.

Limassol, in the south of the island, is a bustling town with ten miles of coastline filled with restaurants, tavernas and night spots. It is home to two popular annual events, the Carnival and the Wine Festival.

Nicosia Photo: Christos Violaris

Limassol port Photo:Cyprus Tourism Organisation

Larnaka sea – front

Larnaka Municipal Cultural Centre

Larnaka

The coastal town of Larnaka, in the southeast, has a population of 79 000 and is the island's second commercial port and also a popular tourist resort. The Larnaka International Airport is situated to the south of the city.

The birthplace of the philosopher Zenon, Larnaka is famous for its Palm Tree Promenade overlooking the sea. It was in Larnaka that Saint Lazarus came to live after his resurrection by Christ. The Church of Saint Lazarus is a magnificent building.

The town is famous for its annual Festival and Fair that commemorates the *Kataklysmos* (the Biblical Flood) and involves traditional singing, dancing and other competitions.

Pafos port Photo: Press and Information Office

Pafos

Pafos in the southwest with a population of 52 800 is a fast-developing tourist resort and home to the island's second international airport.

With an abundance of historic sites and fine beaches, the whole town of Pafos is included on the official UNESCO world heritage list of cultural and national treasures.

Famagusta, Keryneia, Morfou

In the Turkish-occupied areas, Famagusta in the eastern part of the island, was the main port and the centre of the pre-1974 tourist industry. Other main towns under Turkish occupation are Keryneia in the north and Morfou in the northwest.

Places of Interest

Nicosia Area

Nicosia Venetian Walls Photo: Press and Information Office

Venetian Walls

Constructed in 1570 in a perfect circle with eleven bastions around the old town of Nicosia.

Cathedral of Ayios Ioannis Photo: Christos Violaris

Cathedral of Ayios Ioannis

Built in the old part of Nicosia in the seventeenth century with rich fresco paintings that date to the eighteenth century.

Laiki Yeitonia in the old part of Nicosia Photo: Cyprus Tourism Organisation

Laiki Yeitonia

Part of the old town of Nicosia, restored, with restaurants galleries and souvenir shops.

Laiki Yeitonia in the old part of Nicosia Photo: Press and Information Office

Chryssaliniotissa Church

The oldest Byzantine church in Nicosia, believed to have been built in 1450 by Helena Paleologos.

Omeriye Mosque

A medieval Augustian monastery turned into a mosque since the sixteenth century.

The Omeriye Mosque Photo: Press and Information Office

Chryssaliniotissa Crafts Centre

A complex of workshops for traditional and modern Cypriot crafts such as glassware, woodwork e.t.c.

Working artist at the Chryssaliniotissa Crafts Centre Photo: Press and Information Office

Ancient city – Kingdom of Idalion

The area where according to mythology Adonis, lover of Aphrodite, was killed by a wild boar sent by her jealous husband.

Asinou Church

Restored with the help of UNESCO, the church was originally built over eight hundred years ago. Its magnificent frescoes have retained their brilliance of color.

The Byzantine Church of Asinou   Photo: Press and Information Office

Church of Ayios Nikolaos tis Stegis

A good examle of Byzantine architecture dating to the eleventh century, covered with frescoes. The church is included in UNESCO's list of World Heritage.

The Church of Ayios Nicolaos tis Stegis, included in UNESCO's list of World Heritage
Photo: Cyprus Tourism Organisation

Kykkos Monastery   Photo: Press and Information Office

Kykkos Monastery

It houses a monastery collection going back to the time of the Emperor Alexios I Comnenos (1081 – 1118). One icon of the Virgin Mary kept in the monastery is considered the holiest on the island. The mausoleum of Archbishop Makarios III is at a short distance from the monastery.

Village of Fikardou

It received the EUROPA NOSTRA Award in 1987 for the restoration of some of its houses, excellent examples of rural eighteenth century Cypriot architecture. The whole village has been declared a monument.

Village of Fikardou (Europa Nostra Award 1987)   Photo: Press and Information Office

Limassol Mediaeval Fort Photo: Press and Information Office

Limassol Mediaeval Fort
Near the town's old port, it is the place where Richard the Lionheart is said to have married Berengaria of Navarre and crowned her Queen of England in 1191. It houses the Cyprus Mediaeval Museum.

St. Nicholas of the Cats Monastery
The Monastery was founded in 325 A.D. by St. Helen, mother of Emperor Constantine the Great. The present church and monastery are built on Gothic ruins of the thirteenth century when the church was rebuilt.

Amathous
One of the ancient city- kingdoms of Cyprus, situated east of the town of Limassol, with ruins from the Archaic, Roman and Christian Periods.

Amathous, one of the ancient city – kingdoms of Cyprus Photo: Cyprus Tourism Organisation

Kolossi Castle Photo: Press and Information Office

Kolossi Castle
Originally built in the thirteenth century and rebuilt in the fifteenth century in its present form, it served as the Grand Commandery of the Knights of the Order of St. John of Jerusalem. It later came under the domain of the Knights Templar. It is situated west of Limassol on the road to Pafos.

The ancient theatre of Kourion, 50-175 A.D. **Photo: Press and Information Office**

Kourion

Situated west of Limassol, Kourion was an ancient city-kingdom of Cyprus. Its Greco-Roman theatre, built in the second century B.C., has been fully restored and is used for various performances. With its mosaic floors, the Stadium and other ruins, it is a spectacular archaeological site.

Church of Ayios Lazaros, Larnaka **Photo: Press and Information Office**

Church of Ayios Lazaros

A fine example of Byzantine architecture, it was built in the ninth century by Emperor Leo VI over the tomb of Saint Lazarus. The tomb is still under the sanctuary. The church was restored in the seventeenth century and its iconostasis is a unique example of baroque wood carving.

Kition

It is one of Cyprus' city-kingdoms and its ruins date back to the thirteenth century B.C. It was rebuilt by the Mycenaean Greeks in about 1200 B.C.

Larnaka Fort

Built in 1625 on Larnaka's waterfront, it was used as a prison during the first years of British rule. It now houses the Larnaka Mediaeval Museum and the Larnaka Municipal Cultural Centre.

Church of Panayia Angeloktisti

Built in the eleventh century over the ruins of an Early Christian basilica, this Byzantine church is situated in the village of Kiti, west of Larnaka. A sixth century mosaic of the Virgin Mary and Child between the two Archangels from the original building, rivals the Ravenna Mosaics.

Hala Sultan mosque, Larnaka   **Photo: Press and Information Office**

Hala Sultan Mosque

Situated near Larnaka Airport, this mousque was built in 1815 over the tomb of Umm Haram, a relative of the Prophet Mohammed. Today it is an important place of worship for Moslems living in Cyprus.

Khirokitia

One of the most important Neolithic settlements dating to 7000 B.C.,

Church of Panayia Angeloktisti, Kiti   **Photo: Press and Information Office**

Ancient Khirokitia   **Photo: Cyprus Tourism Organisation**

Replicas of the original round houses at the site of ancient Khirokitia

it is situated off the Nicosia – Limassol road. Replicas of the original round houses have been constructed.

Kalavassos – Tenta

Neolithic settlement, near the village of Kalavassos.

Lefkara

Famous for its lace and silverware, Lefkara is a picturesque village off the Nicosia – Limassol road. Legend has it that Leonardo da Vinci visited the village and bought an altar cloth which he donated to the Milan Cathedral.

Street in the village of Lefkara with lace and silver shops

Pafos Area

"Ganymides and the Eagle", Pafos Mosaics

The Mosaics of Pafos

These mosaic floors, depicting scenes from Greek mythology, date from the third to the fifth centuries. On the site of Nea Pafos, the mosaics decorate the floors of four luxurious villas, ruins of the old city of Pafos.

"Apollo and Marcias" , Pafos Mosaics

Tombs of the Kings, Pafos Photo: Cyprus Tourism Organisation

Tombs of the Kings

Dating back to the fourth century B.C., these underground tombs are carved out of solid rock.

Sanctuary of Aphrodite

One of the main pilgrimage centres used until the fourth century, it is situated on the site of the old city-kingdom of Palaepafos

Petra tou Romiou, birthplace of Aphrodite Photo: Press and Information Office

Petra tou Romiou

Legend says that Aphrodite rose from the waves at this place. The name, Petra tou Romiou, the 'Rock of the Greek', refers to the legendary frontier-guard of the Byzantine Empire Digenis Akritas. According to tradition, he heaved a large rock into the sea and destroyed a Saracen ship.

Ayios Neophytos Monastery

Twetfth century monastery founded at the north of Pafos by the Cypriot hermit and writer Neophytos. Well preserved Byzantine

Ayios Neophytos Monastery, commonly called the Encleistra Photo: Press and Information Office

Fresco, a scene from the Passion of Christ, 1503,
Ayios Neophytos Monastery

frescoes can be seen in the Encleistra, the rock chapel carved out of the mountain. One of these frescoes carries the signature of the earliest Byzantine painter known by name.

Chysorogiatissa Monastery

Founded in the twelfth century, the monastery has a collection of icons and other treasures, while its winery produces vintage wine.

Chrysorogiatissa Monastery, Pafos Area

Polis tis Chrysochous

A popular resort with wonderful clear beaches, 37 kilometres north of Pafos.

Baths of Aphrodite

Situated on the road from Pafos to Polis, it is a natural grotto with a pool where according to tradition Aphrodite used to bathe.

Baths of Aphrodite

Akamas Photo: Cyprus Tourism Organisation

Akamas Peninsula

Also called The Last Wilderness of Cyprus, it is inaccessible except by four-wheel drive vehicles. Dirt roads, unspoiled beaches, nature hikes, rare plant species and a nature reserve for endangered green and loggerhead turtles at Lara beach are part of this region of breathtaking beauty.

Akamas Photo: Press and Information Office

Church of Prophet Elias, Paralimni – Protaras Photo: Christos Violaris

Nissi Beach, Ayia Napa Photo: Press and Information Office

Ayia Napa/Protaras

Major coastal resorts boasting lovely beaches and exciting night-life.

Fishing shelter, Potamos Liopetriou

Potamos Liopetriou

A fishing shelter where French poet Arthur Rimbaud worked in the 1880s.

Cape Greco

Cape Greco

An attractive spot for scuba divers, with beaches and coves and a rugged shoreline.

Climate

Cyprus is the warmest island in the Mediterranean. The mean daily temperature in July and August ranges between 29°C on the central plain to 22°C on the Troodos mountains, while the average maximum temperature for these months ranges between 36°C and 27°C, respectively. Winters are generally quite mild. On average, the island enjoys more than three hundred days of sunshine a year, and precipitation tends to be confined to the period between November and March. Snow occurs rarely in the lowlands and on the northern range of Keryneia, but falls every winter (usually December through April) in areas above 1 000 metres on the Troodos Range.

Troodos mountains dressed in white

Photo: Press and Information Office

Vegetation and Flora

In antiquity, Cyprus was widely known as the Green Island because most of the island, even the Messaoria central plain which is almost completely treeless today, was covered with extensive forests. Over the centuries, however, forest vegetation has dramatically been reduced in extent and quality due to human and other influences such as expansion of cultivation, human settlement, misuse and overexploitation, intensive grazing, fires and climatic changes.

Considerable forests still exist along the Troodos and Pentadaktylos Ranges and along the coast of the Akamas peninsula in the west, the Akrotiri peninsula in the south, Cape Greco in the southeast, the Karpassia peninsula in the east, as well as along the northern coasts. The central Messaoria plain, which is classified as a semi-arid zone, has no forest vegetation other than high shrub.

Flora

In relation to its size, Cyprus' flora is one of the richest in the Mediterranean region. This is due to the country's geological structure, climatic conditions, geography, its insular character, and topographical configuration. Extensive plains, mountain masses, wetlands, coasts, sand dunes, gorges and cliffs provide a home for many indigenous and endemic species.

The number of indigenous plant taxa (species subspecies, varieties, hybrids and forms) recorded until now in Cyprus exceeds 1900, as shown below:

Trees 52
Shrubs 131
Sub shrubs 88
Herbs 1637

Total 1908

The Cyprus flora includes a comparatively high proportion of endemic plants amounting to about 140, or 7.34 percent of the total number of native plants. Another important constituent of the indigenous flora are plants typical of the Eastern Mediterranean region, many of

Bosea cypria

Cedrus brevifolia

Colchicum troodi

Crocus cyprius

Crocus hermoneus

which are known as near-endemics because they occur only in two or three countries in the world.

The main habitats of the endemic and other important plants of Cyprus are included in areas proposed as "Natura 2000" sites, as part of the European network of protected areas. These areas will be managed and monitored based on the prescriptions of formal management plans targeting the effective protection of the floral diversity and habitats in such areas. Some of the most important of

Euphorbia thompsonii

Pinguicula

these areas with outstanding floristic richness are the Akamas peninsula, the Pafos Forest, the National Forest Park of Troodos, the Cape Greco National Forest Park and the Larnaka and Akrotiri salt lakes.

The flora of Cyprus is threatened by a number of factors which are common to several countries worldwide. The principal threats are habitat loss, change in land use, abandonment, tourist development, expansion of built-up areas, drying up of watercourses and climatic

Quercus alnifolia (Golden Oak)

Photo: Forestry Department

change. The Red Data List for the island's flora compiled in 2003 indicates that about 300 plant species are faced with extinction, and, at least for some, immediate protection measures are required.

The best period of the year to study the native flora, especially the herbaceous plants, is spring, but also winter in the lowlands, where the flowering season begins early with the first rains. On the mountains and along main streams this period is extended.

Tulipa cypria
Photo: Forestry Department

Exotic and Cultivated Plants

A large number of ornamental trees and shrubs have been introduced in Cyprus, especially during the last century. Some of these exotic plants, particularly acacias and eucalyptus, have been so extensively planted, especially in the lowlands, that today they are characteristic of the lowlands of the island. Other exotic species with significant occurrence are several species of pine trees.

Cultivated plants on the lowlands include cereals, irrigated crops of various vegetables (potatoes, tomatoes, etc.), whereas citrus species are commonly cultivated along the coastal zone. Olive, carob, and almond trees constitute a major component of cultivated plants at low and mid altitudes. At medium altitudes, vineyards are dominant in many places, especially in the Limassol and Pafos Districts. At higher elevations, in addition to vineyards, there are orchards of apple, cherry and peach trees.

Forests

The forests of Cyprus are an important national resource, but the forest sector is subject to pressures from many directions to which it has to respond. Forests provide timber and non-wood products; more importantly, they contribute significantly to the beauty of the

Pinus brutia forest, Troodos mountains
Photo: Forestry Department

Nature and People | **91**

landscape, preservation of the national heritage, protection of water supplies, rural life, village communities and the general well-being of Cypriot citizens; they attract visitors from abroad on whom the national economy is heavily dependent. The future prosperity of the country is to some extent bound up with its forests and what happens to them. With effective conservation and sound management, forest resources offer multidimensional opportunities for socioeconomic development, especially in rural areas.

Forest areas on the island account for 42.3 percent of the total land area. High forests make up the 43.8 percent, whereas *maquis* and lower vegetation account for 56.2 percent of the island's total forest.

Cedar valley, Troodos mountains **Photo: Forestry Department**

Black pine forest, Troodos mountains **Photo: Forestry Department**

Maquis *forest*

Photo: Forestry Department

Fauna

The rich nature of Cyprus, specifically its fauna and flora, is mainly the result of species evolution over time, under the influence of climate and soil conditions, the island's geographic position and insular character—hence its relative isolation—and the human influence in relation to the limited extent of the land.

The diversity of landscapes with their special microclimatic and topographical features, the soil and geological diversity, the variety of vegetation associations, and forest and agricultural plant species, create a variety of ecological niches and habitats capable of meeting the biological needs of a large number of animal species.

Presently, about 30 mammal species, 25 reptiles and amphibians, 370 bird species, 250 fish species and approximately 6 000 insect species are known to live in various habitats of the island.

Mammals

Archaeological evidence shows that various big mammals, like elephants and hippopotami, used to live on the island thousands of years ago. Due to the absence of enemies and their special feeding habits, these species gradually evolved into pygmies adapting to the environment. Shortly after the first humans settled on Cyprus, eight to ten thousand years ago, these species disappeared, obviously as a result of intensive hunting. Skeletons of the pygmy elephant and hippopotamus have recently been found in caves in the Akrotiri area.

During the Neolithic and Chalcolithic Periods, new mammal species appeared on the island, such as the Mesopotamian deer, the Fallow deer, the Red deer, the Marten, the wild cat, the fox, the mouflon, the hare and various mice species.

Some mammal species were brought to Cyprus as domestic animals by the first settlers of the island. Many of them escaped and lived in the wild, but eventually became extinct after intensive hunting. A few species have survived until today.

Bones of Mesopotamian deer were found in a number of areas on the island, an indication that this species was widespread. It became

extinct relatively recently, probably four hundred years ago, almost certainly as a result of continuous hunting.

The mouflon is a species of wild sheep endemic to Cyprus. It is the biggest wild mammal of the island and is a real treasure of the Cyprus forests. It is believed to have come to Cyprus as a domestic animal around 8000 B.C. with the first human arrivals. In the past, it was common on both Troodos and Pentadaktylos. However, uncontrolled hunting led to a dramatic decrease of the mouflon population. During the 1930s, there were only fifteen animals left which found refuge in the Pafos forest. In view of the high risk of extinction, the whole Pafos state forest was designated a game reserve, and the mouflon population recovered. Today it numbers in the thousands.

Cyprus fox – Vulpes vulpes indutus   **Photo: Forestry Department**

The fox is an endemic subspecies and the only carnivorous mammal of the island. It can be found in many areas even though its population has been constantly declining over the last two decades. Ecologists consider the fox a useful animal with an important role in the ecosystems.

Cyprus mouflon – Ovis gmelini ophion
Photo: Forestry Department

Long-eared hedgehog – Hemiechinus auritus dorotheae　　Photo: Forestry Department

The hare is also an endemic subspecies. It is the main and biggest game species in Cyprus. It can be found everywhere on the island in fairly large numbers.

The hedgehog is another endemic subspecies of Cyprus. It is a nocturnal, shy species found in suitable habitats at 1 600 metres above sea level.

Egyptian Fruitbat – Rousettus aegyptiacus　　Photo: Forestry Department

The bat species is one of the most strange but important animal groups of the Cyprus fauna. There are sixteen bat species on the island. So far, very few studies have been conducted on their biology. Their role in the ecosystem is vital since they feed mainly on insects, and only the fruit bat feeds on mature fruits.

Birds

Due to its geographical position, Cyprus is one of the most important migratory routes in Europe. It is also considered as an area with rich avifauna, and an important bird area in Europe with high endemism.

Barn owl – Tyto alba　　Photo: Forestry Department

The number of bird species recorded until now in Cyprus is 370. Of those, 53 are permanent residents, while the remaining 317 are migrants. Of the migratory birds, 237 are common visitors and the remaining 80 are rare or quite rare visitors. The number of the

Cyprus wheatear – Oenanthe cypriaca　　Photo: Forestry Department

Grey heron – Ardea cinerrea

Long eared owl – Asio otus

Photo: Forestry Department

migratory birds visiting Cyprus in a year depends on the climatic conditions of Northern and Eastern Europe as well as on the amount of precipitation that falls on the island in a given year.

The total number of breeding birds in Cyprus is 114. Six of the permanent residents are endemic (two species and four subspecies), as follows:

Cyprus warbler
Cyprus wheatear
Tree creeper
Jay
Scops owl
Coal tit

European Roller – Coracias garrulus Photo: Forestry Department

Migration is a phenomenon repeated nearly the same period every year. Weather conditions during migration both in autumn and spring are characterised by light winds, perfect visibility and low cloud cover, conditions that are favourable for birds during their migration journeys from Europe to Africa and back.

Reptiles and Amphibians

There are twenty-two reptile and three amphibian species living in Cyprus. They include three turtle species, eleven species of lizards (four endemic subspecies) and eight snake species, which include one endemic species and two endemic subspecies. Three of the snakes found in Cyprus are poisonous but only one can be harmful to humans.

Frog – Bufo viridis Photo: Forestry Department

Three frog species are included among the amphibians: the tree frog, the marsh frog and the green toad.

Pond turtle – Mauremis caspica Photo: Forestry Department

The native turtle species include two marine species, the green turtle and the common turtle (*Caretta caretta*), which visit the sandy beaches of Cyprus to lay their eggs. The third turtle species is the European pond turtle, which is endangered on the island because of habitat loss and the drying up of rivers. The species lives in rivulets with low water speed and rich vegetation cover in near Nicosia and Polis tis Chrysochou.

Agama lizard – Lanudakia stellio cypriaca   **Photo: Forestry Department**

One of the most interesting and rare lizards is the berber skink, a very fast reptile with a body length of 30-40 centimetres.

A very common reptile is the agama lizard. It is also very fast and lives in a wide range of habitats with dry conditions.

The endemic Cyprus whip snake is found mainly in the Pafos forest. It has a long, thin body with a length of about 75 centimetres. Its colour is dark grey or black. It is not a poisonous snake and feeds mainly on lizards. It was identified as an endemic species in 1983.

The large whip snake is the most common snake of the island. It is not poisonous and its colour is black. It is a very well-known snake which can live even in gardens, keeping them clear from other snakes and mice, as it feeds on them. A very common snake is the blunt-nosed viper. It is the most dangerous snake of the island with a powerful venom.

Grass snake – Natrix natrix cypriaca   **Photo: Forestry Department**

Two rare snakes of the island are the cat snake and the grass snake, which was rediscovered in 1992 after thirty years with no records. Confined to four locations on the island, it is strictly protected.

Butterfly – Charaxes jasius

Insects

Scientific knowledge on insect species is comparatively poor in Cyprus, with the exception of certain groups like butterflies and insects with agricultural interest. Up-to-date records and studies indicate that the number of insects presently known to exist in Cyprus is about 6000. Butterflies constitute one of the most important groups of insects. There are fifty-two butterfly species in Cyprus, of which nine are endemic. Several other insect species are also endemic. The most important habitats of those species are protected.

Green juvenile turtle

Turtles and Turtle Conservation in Cyprus

Of marine turtles, two breed regularly on the island's beaches, the Green Turtle (*Chelonia mydas*) and the Loggerhead Turtle (*Caretta caretta*). Both species were more abundant in the past. Though records are sparse, old fishermen attest to this, as does the toponymy of at least one area, Chelones (turtles), a fisherman's cove in the Karpassia peninsula adjoining an area of extensive sandy beaches stretching to Cape Andreas. Leatherback turtles (*Dermochelys coriacea*) are also occasionally found in the waters of Cyprus, although no nesting activity of this species has been noted anywhere in the Mediterranean.

By the middle of the twentieth century, rampant exploitation decimated turtle populations in the Mediterranean. Tens of thousands of turtles were shipped, mainly between 1900 and 1960, from the Eastern Mediterranean to Europe, where there was a great demand for turtle soup. Currently, intensive use of beaches for tourism and recreational purposes is threatening turtles in the Mediterranean by depriving them of their nesting grounds. Many turtles drown or are killed when caught in fishing nets or on lines. As a result, turtles, especially the Green Turtles, are on the verge of extinction in the Mediterranean. It is estimated that the current nesting population of turtles is about 500-600 female Green turtles and about 5 000-6 000 Loggerhead turtles.

The World Conservation Union (IUCN) has declared both Green and Loggerhead turtles as endangered, the Mediterranean Green Turtle as critically so. Both species are protected under the Council of Europe's Convention on the Conservation of European Wildlife and Natural Habitats (Bern Convention) and under the Barcelona Convention (UNEP). An Action Plan for their conservation has been approved by Mediterranean States within the Mediterranean Action Plan. Finally, the Convention on Migratory Species (CMS) and the Convention on International Trade in Endangered Species (CITES) also protect turtles. Cyprus has ratified these conventions.

A project to help the marine turtles of Cyprus was launched in 1978 by the Fisheries Department. The project, which includes a seasonal station and a hatchery at Lara, is financed by the Cyprus Government. In 1980, it received World Wildlife Fund support for three years, as an IUCN/WWF project, and in 1990 it received assistance from the European Union as a MEDSPA Project (Mediterranean Special Programme Action). The Cyprus Turtle Conservation Project is the first of its kind in the Mediterranean.

The main thrust of the project aims at:

- Protecting and managing turtle nesting beaches
- Protecting eggs and hatchlings from predation and human activities
- Protecting adult turtles
- Monitoring the turtle population and nesting activity in Cyprus
- Raising public awareness in turtle conservation.

Thorough surveys of the turtle nesting beaches in 1976 and 1977 showed that Green Turtles were breeding on several beaches, including those of Ayia Napa and the unspoilt surf-swept west coast beaches north of Pafos. Since then, nesting at Ayia Napa and on some beaches in Pafos has ceased due to a sharp increase in tourism or because the beaches were degraded by sand extraction. Loggerheads nest on the same beaches as the Greens and also on the extensive beaches of Chrysochou Bay (mainly in the Polis/Limni/Yialia area), which are their main nesting area. Regular but less dense or occasional nesting also takes place on a number of other beaches.

Training course at Lara Reserve

Turtles are an ancient group of reptiles which, like marine mammals such as dolphins, seals and whales, have reversed their evolution and returned to the sea. This reverse process is, however, incomplete, and though turtles have adapted well to life at sea—they are excellent swimmers and can stay underwater for long periods—their ties to their land-adapted ancestors are unmistakable. Turtles still have to breathe air and come up on land to lay their eggs.

Lara beach with station

Turtles lay eggs every two to five years. Loggerheads nest mainly from the end of May to about the middle of August, while Greens start and finish about two weeks later. During the breeding season, they lay eggs three to five times, every two weeks. Loggerheads lay about 80 eggs per clutch, while Greens lay on average 120 eggs. Loggerheads lay their eggs in chambers about 40-50 centimetres deep, while Greens lay theirs deeper, at about 50-80 centimetres.

Turtle hatchlings are attracted to lights. The hatchlings emerge from the sand at night, about seven weeks after the eggs are laid. They head directly for the sea. Their instinctive location of the sea is based on their attraction to the lightest part of the horizon—

Green turtle (Chelonia Mydas), on nesting beach in Lara Reserve

which is normally the sea. Hatchlings will, however, be attracted to artificial lights near the nesting beach. If they get disorientated and go towards such lights, instead of quickly going to the sea, they increase their chances of falling prey to foxes. If they remain on land during the day they soon die of the heat. Nesting females are shy and wary of lights and movement on the beaches when they come up to lay their eggs. If disturbed, they go straight back to the safety of the sea—interrupting their nesting. If disturbed on consecutive nights, they will drop their eggs in the sea. This is why the public is not allowed on nesting beaches at night. Deep car tyre grooves on beaches also misdirect hatchlings, which can follow the tracks for hundreds of metres, thereby placing themselves in danger.

Surveys during the early stages of the project at Polis/Limni revealed that more than 80 percent of the eggs were found dug up and eaten by foxes. Once the hatchlings reach the sea, they face new enemies. Predation is, however, natural, yet for thousands of years enough hatchlings reached the sea and survived to keep a stable population. It is human interference that has caused their demise. To counteract this, control of predation has been undertaken so as to increase the number of hatchlings reaching the sea. Some eggs are laid too near the water and perish by being covered by waves during high tide or storms.

In the Lara-Toxeftra Reserve and on the Polis-Limni beaches, all nests are protected *in situ*, i.e., where the eggs were laid, by placing special aluminium cages over them. These allow the hatchlings to escape to the sea as soon as they emerge from the sand, but prevent foxes from getting at the nest. A hatchery is used for a small number of nests that cannot be adequately protected. The hutchery is a fenced off part of the beach where eggs are transferred and reburied. The eggs have to be buried at the right depth as sex determination in turtles is dependent on the incubation temperature. Incubation at 29°-30°C results in half the hatchlings being male and the other half female. Lower temperatures result in male hatchlings. Higher temperatures produce females. This

*Loggerhead (*Caretta Caretta*) hatchlings, heading for the sea at dawn at Lara Reserve*

means that eggs laid early in the season are more likely to produce male hatchlings than eggs laid later on. A number of nests, laid too near the sea and prone to inundation by waves, are relocated higher up on the same beach.

Though there are fluctuations in the number of turtles nesting from year to year, on average about 8 000 hatchlings of both species are released every year from the Lara-Toxeftra Reserve area. In addition, over 12 000 Loggerhead hatchlings reach the sea from protected nests on the Chrysochou Bay beaches. These numbers are many times the number that would normally reach the sea if the nests were not protected.

The breeding population of Green Turtles is about 100 females, nesting mailnly in the Lara-Toxeftra area (105 females have been tagged so far). The Loggerhead population is somewhat larger and has been estimated at about 300 females. Turtles are tagged and their reappearance on the nesting beaches is monitored.

Though the time required for turtles to reach maturity is still uncertain, it is estimated that Loggerheads mature at about 15-20 years and Greens at about 25-35 years. Turtles imprint on the beaches on which they incubate and hatch. When mature they find their way back to the same beaches to lay their own eggs. The imprinting mechanism is based on a variety of clues, among which are geomagnetic forces (hence the use of aluminium cages for nest protection). Therefore, all precautions are taken to disturb as little as possible the hatchlings' incubation and first descent to the sea, a critical time for their survival.

Raising turtles to larger sizes and releasing them has also been researched. Several hundred, mainly Green Turtles, ranging from one to ten years old, were kept in sea cages in Pafos harbour and in special tanks in Nicosia. These were released at various ages. Pending results from this head-start experiment, further rearing of turtles has been suspended, as it is not clear if the benefits from such rearing outweigh the dangers involved.

In Cyprus, turtles and their eggs have been protected by law since 1971, along with dolphins and seals (regulations made under the Fisheries Law). In 1989 the Lara-Toxeftra coastal region and adjacent sea was declared, under the same law, a Protected Area, and is managed as such by the Department of Fisheries and Marine Research. It covers a stretch of coastline 10 kilometres long, from the location known as Aspros, near Ayios Georghios, to Argaki tou Yousouphi, about three kilometres north of Lara. This includes the main beaches from Toxeftra to the north Lara bay. The sea area protected stretches to the 20-metre isobath, which is about 1.5 kilometres from the shore. The management measures aim at avoiding human interference with the breeding activity during nesting , incubation and hatching.

Regardless of the successful increase of young turtles into the population, the long-term prospects for the survival of the turtles, without habitat protection, are, at best, doubtful. As turtles return to their natal beaches to reproduce, they form local populations, the survival of which depends on their protection on those particular beaches. In other words, protecting turtles in one area/country will not help turtles in another area. Currently, the Mediterranean Green Turtle nests mainly in Cyprus and on a few beaches in Turkey and sparsely in Israel. Its breeding activity in other neighbouring countries has practically ceased or is only occasional. Loggerhead Turtles in the Mediterranean nest mainly in Greece, Turkey and Cyprus. Some nesting also takes place in Libya (now being assessed) and Israel, while sparse nesting takes place also in Egypt, Lebanon, Syria and Tynisia and on some southern Italian islands.

Since 1989, there have been annual training courses in Turtle Conservation Techniques and Beach Management for Mediterranean scientists and Protected Area managers for the United Nations Environment Programme (RAC/SPA of the Mediterranean Action Plan). The Cyprus Wildlife Society, which helps with the project, holds these courses in cooperation with the Department of Fisheries and Marine Research.

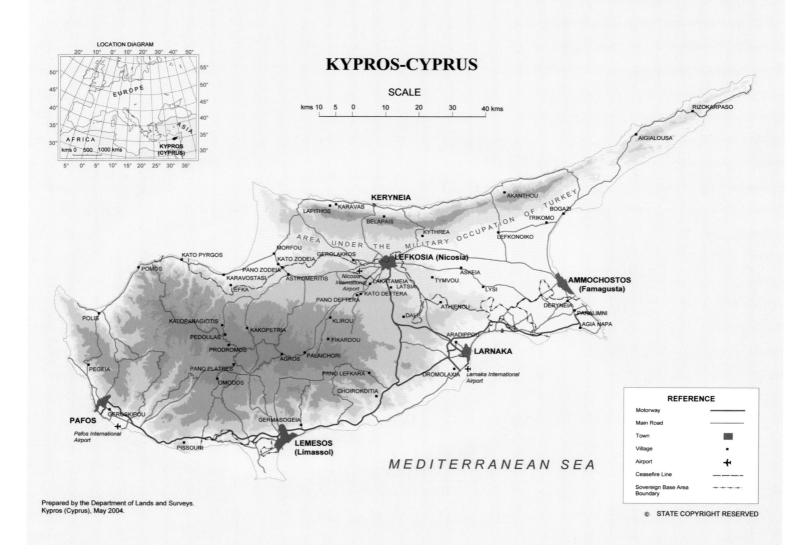

KYPROS-CYPRUS

LOCATION DIAGRAM

EUROPE

ASIA

AFRICA

KYPROS (CYPRUS)

SCALE

kms 10 5 0 10 20 30 40 kms

KERYNEIA

LAPITHOS · KARAVAS

BELAPAIS

AKANTHOU

BOGAZI

TRIKOMO

KYTHREA

LEFKONOIKO

AREA UNDER THE MILITARY OCCUPATION OF TURKEY

RIZOKARPASO

AIGIALOUSA

MORFOU

KATO PYRGOS

KATO ZODEIA

GEROLAKKOS

POMOS

PANO ZODEIA

KARAVOSTASI

ASTROMERITIS

LEFKA

LEFKOSIA (Nicosia)

Nicosia International Airport

LAKATAMEIA

LATSIA

KATO DEFTERA

ASKEIA

TYMVOU

LYSI

AMMOCHOSTOS (Famagusta)

POLIS

KALOPANAGIOTIS

PANO DEFTERA

KLIROU

FIKARDOU

ATHIENOU

DALI

DERYNEIA

PARALIMNI

AGIA NAPA

PEDOULAS

KAKOPETRIA

ARADIPPOU

PEGEIA

PRODROMOS

AGROS

PALAICHORI

PANO PLATRES

PANO LEFKARA

LARNAKA

PAFOS

GEROSKIPOU

Pafos International Airport

OMODOS

CHOIROKOITIA

DROMOLAXIA

Larnaka International Airport

PISSOURI

GERMASOGEIA

LEMESOS (Limassol)

MEDITERRANEAN SEA

REFERENCE

Motorway	
Main Road	
Town	■
Village	▪
Airport	✈
Ceasefire Line	
Sovereign Base Area Boundary	

Prepared by the Department of Lands and Surveys.
Kypros (Cyprus), May 2004.

© STATE COPYRIGHT RESERVED

Global Affiliate

On the International Scene

In the European Union

On the International Scene

The Republic of Cyprus became an independent sovereign state on 16 August 1960. Soon thereafter it became a member of the United Nations, the Commonwealth, the Non-Aligned Movement and the Council of Europe. It subsequently became a member of other international organisations, including the Organisation on Security and Cooperation in Europe, formally the Conference on Security and Cooperation in Europe.

On 1 May 2004, Cyprus became a member of the European Union.

Photo: United Nations Archives

United Nations

Cyprus has been a member of the United Nations since 20 September 1960.

The Security Council, the General Assembly and other bodies of the United Nations, including the Commission on Human Rights, the Sub-

President Papadopoulos addresses the UN General Assembly, 25.9.2003

Photo: Athens News Agency

Commission on Prevention of Discrimination and Protection of Minorities, the Committee on the Elimination of Racial Discrimination, UNESCO) have over the years dealt with the Cyprus Question and adopted numerous resolutions on all its aspects.

Council of Europe

Cyprus has been a member of the Council of Europe since May 1961 and participates in all its bodies and organs, including the Parliamentary Assembly. Cypriot experts participate in most of the Council's specialised Committees, where their contribution has been widely acknowledged.

The Council, responding to Cyprus' applications, has found Turkey, based on relevant reports of the European Commission of Human Rights, guilty of serious violations of the European Convention on Human Rights in the part of Cyprus occupied by Turkey. Also, in a landmark decision on 10 May 2001 the European Court of Human Rights of the Council of Europe found Turkey guilty of gross violations of human rights in Cyprus as a result of the 1974 invasion. In a judgment passed by sixteen votes to one—the dissenting vote of Turkey—the Strasbourg Court ruled that Turkey has violated fourteen articles of the European Convention on Human Rights involving, inter alia, the living conditions of the Greek Cypriots enclaved in the occupied areas of the island, Turkey's refusal to investigate the fate of

Parliamentary Assembly of the Council of Europe

the missing persons, and the right of the displaced persons to return to their homes. Moreover, in another judgment on 18 December 1996 concerning the case of Titina Loizidou, a Greek Cypriot, the European Court of Human Rights held that the denial to the applicant of access to her property in the Turkish-occupied territories of Cyprus and the loss of control of her property was imputable to Turkey and its subordinate local administration. In fact, the European Court of Human Rights ruled that Loizidou remains the legal owner of her property in Keryneia, and that, by not allowing her access to her property, Turkey is in violation of the European Convention for the Protection of Human Rights.

Organisation on Security and Cooperation in Europe (OSCE)

Cyprus is one of the thirty-five signatory states of the Helsinki Final Act concluded in 1975 and an active participant in the process of the Conference on Security and Cooperation in Europe (CSCE), which on 1 January 1995 became an international organisation under the name Organisation on Security and Cooperation in Europe (OSCE). Cyprus was a founding member of the group of the Neutral and Non-aligned countries, which assumed the role of bridge-building between the opposing interests of East and West.

Cyprus and the Commonwealth

Chief Emeka Anyaokou addresses the opening ceremony of the CHOGM in Nicosia, 1993

Photo: Press and Information Office

Cyprus became a member of the Commonwealth in 1961 and has been actively participating in all Commonwealth activities which cover cooperation in various fields.

Cyprus hosted the Commonwealth Heads of Government Meeting (CHOGM) in 1993 in Limassol. This is indicative of Cyprus' continued commitment to cooperation and a manifestation of the esteem that Cyprus enjoys within the Commonwealth.

The Commonwealth has consistently supported Cyprus in its struggle for a just and viable solution to the Cyprus problem.

Cyprus and the Non-Aligned Movement

The Presidential Palace   **Photo: Press and Information Office**

After its accession to the EU, Cyprus withdrew from the Non-Aligned Movement (NAM), because membership in the EU does not permit simultaneous membership in the NAM. By participating as a guest in future meetings of the NAM in its new capacity as a member of the EU, Cyprus could serve as a bridge between the NAM and the EU, thus enhancing mutual cooperation and understanding between the two.

The NAM has been a constant supporter of a lasting, just and viable solution to the Cyprus Question. NAM's declarations on Cyprus contain all those elements that are important to that end.

Cyprus and the Euro-Mediterranean Partnership

The Euro-Mediterranean Partnership provides the institutional structure for the further development of relations between the European Union and the Mediterranean states. The Partnership was initiated with the Conference of EU and Mediterranean foreign ministers in Barcelona, on 27 and 28 November 1995. This event marked the start of a new partnership phase in relations, including bilateral and multilateral or regional cooperation. Cyprus has participated in the new process since its inception: as a Mediterranean Partner, with Algeria, Egypt, Israel, Jordan, Lebanon, Malta, Morocco, the Palestinian Authority, Syria, Tunisia and Turkey, and since 1 May 2004, as a member of the Union in a Euro-Mediterranean Partnership that numbers thirty-five participating states.

President Tassos Papadopoulos and Foreign Minister George Iacovou sign the Cyprus Accession Treaty, 6 April 2003, Athens

In the European Union

Representation in the EU

Cyprus is represented by one Commissioner in the European Union and by six members in the European Parliament. It has four votes in the EU's policy-making Council of Ministers.

Cypriot President Tassos Papadopoulos addresses the ceremony for the signing of the Accession Treaty of the ten new member-states, 16 April 20003, Athens

EU Leaders in Athens for the signing of the Accession Treaty of the ten new EU member-states, 16 April 2003

Photo: Athens News Agency

European Military Capabilities

As an acceding country, Cyprus will participate in the European Military Capabilities, the EU's rapid reaction force, currently under formation. In view of the Government's proposal for the demilitarisation of the island, Cyprus will not provide combat troops or artillery. It has offered, however, logistics support and auxiliary services to be placed at the disposal of the EU's military force for its crisis management and peace-keeping operations in the region.

What EU Membership Means for Cyprus and Europe

EU membership is the most important challenge facing Cyprus in the twenty-first century. With a modernised economy, Cyprus is ready to be part of a new peaceful and prosperous Europe, in which Greek and Turkish Cypriots together will be ready to take advantage of the vast opportunities that membership offers. The challenge facing Cyprus is to ensure that both communities have a role to play in their country's future.

Membership in the European Union provides the most suitable environment for a fair and lasting settlement on the island, as it will give both Greek and Turkish Cypriots a sense of security and safeguard their fundamental human rights within the framework of the *acquis communautaire* which each member-state must strictly adhere to.

As a result of harmonisation with EU legislation, economic and social reforms have already enhanced and will further improve the living standards of all Cypriot citizens. Social policy is in line with the Social Charter, and greater emphasis will be given to environmental issues and the improvement of safety and quality standards.

EU accession has opened up the world's largest market for Cypriot goods and services and will enable the island to make a positive contribution to the formulation of EU policy.

Cyprus is currently a net contributor to the EU. It will join the Economic and Monetary Union of the EU as of January 2008.

With accession, Cyprus has become the southeastern frontier of the newly-enlarged Europe. The island's geo-strategic position and close proximity to the important oil routes of the area can provide EU countries with access to the large Arab markets and place them at an advantage with respect to their trade and commercial interests. At the same time it provides the Union with a foothold in the Eastern Mediterranean from which to exercise greater economic and political influence and play a leading role in facilitating peace in the region. Cyprus' EU membership will in and by itself bring greater stability and security to the region.

Thanks to Cyprus' mercantile fleet, which ranks as one of the ten largest in the world in terms of gross tonnage, the EU has become the world's largest shipping power.

Because of the island's geographical location, serious problems facing Europe such as illegal immigration, drug trafficking and money laundering can be more effectively monitored and combated.

As a financial and business hub, Cyprus will also afford EU member-states attractive investment opportunities.

Map of Cyprus by Petrius Bertius, Amsterdam 1600

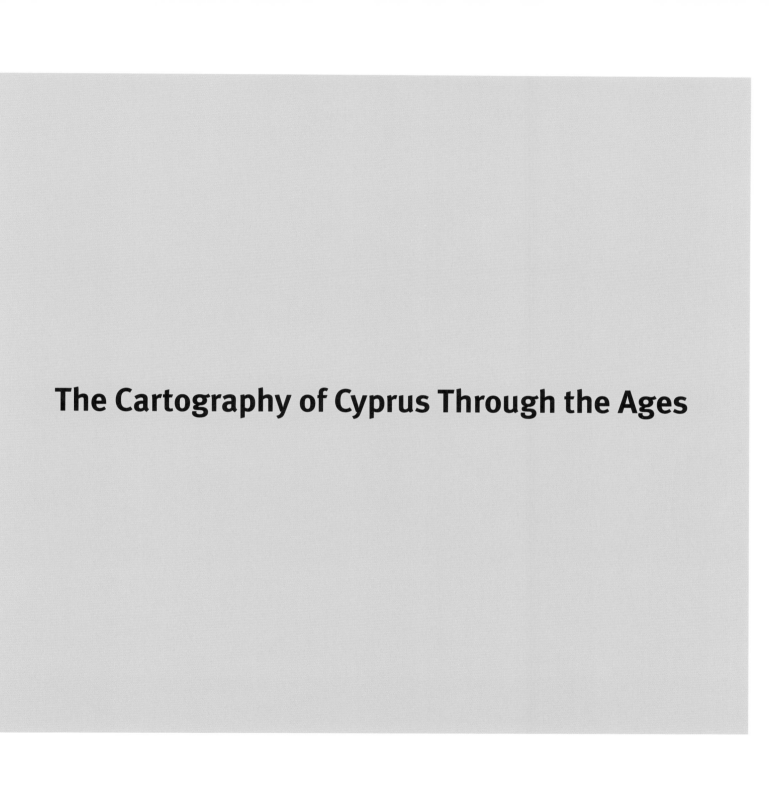

The Cartography of Cyprus Through the Ages

The earliest surviving reference to a map in western literature occurs in the *Histories* of Herodotus and includes Cyprus. Around 500 B.C. Aristagoras, the tyrant of Miletus, showed a bronze tablet to the Spartans depicting "the territories of the Ionians, Lydians, Cappadocians and Cilicians and then enumerated the adjacent seas and indicated the island of Cyprus and finally Susa," the seat of the kings of Persia.

The next Greek to put Cyprus on the map, so to speak, was Strabo (64 B.C.–21 A.D.), who seems to have had considerable knowledge about the island. Based on internal evidence, one may, in fact, presume that Strabo personally toured the island: following his final remarks on the description of Asia Minor, he notes: "We will now tour Cyprus, which is just to the south of this peninsula."

He then goes on to describe in detail the position of Cyprus and the distances between various towns and their relevant position on a map. It must be supposed that he constructed a Cyprus map along with a world map, as he makes a note to that effect in his *Geography*.

To the Romans, who were destined to become masters of most of the known world, Cyprus must have been important. This is why it features prominently, and out of all proportion, on their map, known to us as the Tabula Peutingeriana (Peutinger Map). It occupies the whole of the Eastern Mediterranean between Asia Minor and Egypt.

Claudius Ptolemy

The first man to give a reasonable shape to the geographical features of Cyprus, and for that matter to the whole world, was Claudius Ptolemaeus, known as Ptolemy. This Greek mathematician, astronomer and geographer lived in Roman Egypt during the second century A.D.

Ptolemy's *Geography* is a thorough discussion of the geographic knowledge of the Greco-Roman world. The manuscripts, which are still preserved in libraries today, are from copies of manuscripts that survived due to the diligence of Byzantine scholars. These manuscripts fall into two groups. One version, the A-group, consists of a world map and twenty-six regional maps—ten of Europe, four of Africa and twelve of Asia. It is this set which accompanies the Latin translations made in the fifteenth century and used for the earliest printed editions. Cyprus is shown on the map of the fourth part of Asia, which also includes Syria and Palestine.

The second version, the B-group, contains sixty-four detailed maps of smaller areas. Because of its important position in the Eastern Mediterranean and the Greek world in general, Cyprus was depicted separately as one of the sixty-four areas of the B-group.

By the end of the fifteenth century, Ptolemy could not fully satisfy the demands of Renaissance scholars. For this reason new maps, known as *tabulae novae*, started to appear, together with the old ones in the Geography, displaying new knowledge.

The first printed *tabulae novae* for Cyprus appeared on the map of Asia Minor in the Strasbourg edition of 1513. Cyprus' shape and

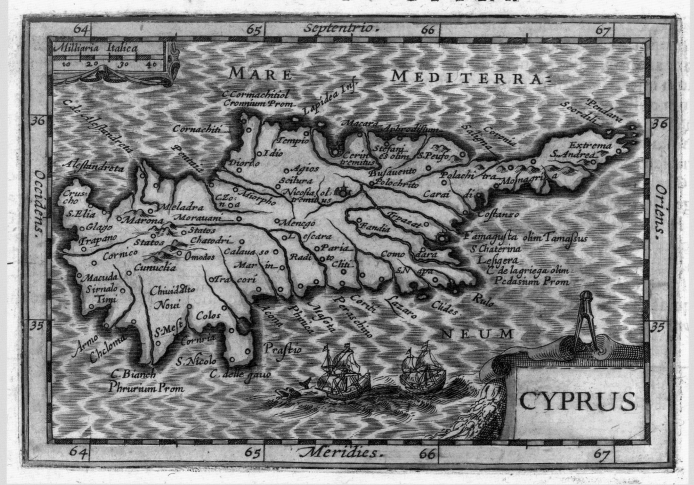

Map of Cyprus by Jodocus Hondius, Amsterdam 1607

contents are a departure from the Ptolemaic tradition. It is obvious that the cartographer, the famous Martin Waldsemuller, used the portolan charts of his period as his sources for Cyprus. The next development in the Cyprus *tabulae novae* series does not appear until several editions later, when the other great cartographer, Giacomo Gastaldi, engraved the maps for the 1548 edition of the *Geography*, and Girolamo Ruscelli edited the edition of 1561 in Venice. These *tabulae novae* provide new information based on Venetian prototypes, but because of the reduced scale, the contents are minimal.

The real development, however, in *tabulae novae* in the editions of Ptolemy comes with the edition of 1596 by Antonio Magini in Venice. Cyprus is given special treatment by Magini and is depicted entirely on its own. It is based on the important map of Cyprus by the Dutch cartographer Ortelius (1573) and referred to in greater detail later.

The Middle Ages

Cyprus does not feature prominently on the *mappae mundi* (the world maps) of the Middle Ages. There was not much naval traveling or campaigning to be done during the Middle Ages, so the island was just a blob on the world map.

As far as Cyprus is concerned, however, a most important source of information on navigation and charting is the Byzantine *Stadiasmos* or *Periplus*. Even more important are the portolan charts on which the island featured prominently because of the existing links between it and Venice and Genoa during the fourteenth century. There is no reason to believe that contemporary chart-makers, or people acting as informants to the Venetian or Genoese chart-makers, actually visited and stayed on the island during this period of portolan chart development.

As drawn in the portolan charts, Cyprus is certainly not the haphazard affair displayed in the medieval *mappae mundi*. The oldest portolan chart existing today, the late–thirteenth-century Carte Pisane, gives reasonable representation of the island, especially of the southern coastline. As regards place names, the *Carte Pisane* includes eleven, which gradually increase to twenty-four in the early-fifteenth-century Venetian charts.

The next development in the mapping of Cyprus comes in the *isolaria*, which were the successors to the portolan charts. The first *isolario* to contain a map of Cyprus was published in manuscript form by Bartolomeo dalli Sonetti in c.1480. The island is presented by itself with the most up-to-date shape and contains sixty-two new medieval place names, some of them inland. Soon after (c.1485), printed editions of the same work appeared. Although we have no direct evidence that dalli Sonetti himself charted Cyprus, we do have a great deal of circumstantial evidence to suggest that he was actually on board the Venetian trireme *Loredana* which, on one of its regular pilgrimages to Jerusalem in 1458, stopped at the island, where several of its passengers met members of the High Court in Nicosia, the capital.

Bartolomeo dalli Sonetti's map of 1480 signalled the renaissance of Cyprus cartography and was the crowning achievement of the gradual development of the sea-chart over several centuries during the Middle Ages.

The Sixteenth Century

During the sixteenth century, several other *isolaria* were also published. Among those that include a map of Cyprus are Benedetto Bordone's *isolario*, published in Venice in 1528, and, later, Camocio's, Donato Bertelli's and S. Pinargenti's, also published in Venice during the 1570s. Tomasso Porcacci's "Isole piu famose del Mondo" was printed in Venice in 1572 and republished on subsequent occasions. These *isolaria* are not notable for any original work as far as Cyprus is concerned.

With the Venetians in possession of the island between 1489 and 1571, Cyprus cartography during the sixteenth century was monopolised by the new rulers, so it is not surprising that the next important and valuable map of the island came from the hands of the well-known Venetian cartographer Matheo Pagano. Working on woodblocks, as was his custom, Pagano published the most up-to-date map of Cyprus in 1538.

The Cypriot chronicler Florio Boustron left a manuscript map of Cyprus c.1560 accompanying his *Chronicle*. The map is important, as it introduces a new shape and is the first to show the

Map of Cyprus by Johann-Matthaeus Merian, 1689-1716

medieval administrative districts of Cyprus. Nicosia appears for the first time on this map with its Greek name Lefkosia. The Cypriot historian Steffano Lusignano's map of 1575/6 cannot, however, claim any originality.

In the mid-sixteenth century there was great activity in the production and publication of loose-sheet maps of Cyprus as well as other parts of the world, the main centres being Venice and Rome. Cyprus maps of this type are those by F. Bertelli, 1562, G. Calapoda Cretensis, 1566 (he copies M. Pagano), C. Duchetti, N. Nelli and A. Lafreri, 1570. Paolo Forlani and Bonifacio Sibenisensis also published maps of Cyprus in Venice in 1570, adding the medieval administrative districts. The most significant loose-sheet map was, however, published by Jacomo Franco c.1570, again in Venice.

Other loose-sheet maps and plans of the period, mostly produced in Germany, were also published as a means of news distribution. These loose sheets were reissued sometimes two or three times a year, each time with the latest information added. Such maps are those by M. Zundt, B. Jenichen and H. Rogel, who published maps of Cyprus to show its invasion by the Turks and the subsequent defeat of the Venetians in 1570/1. Camocio, Bertelli and Pinargenti published similar plans, but theirs have survived in greater numbers as they were preserved, bound into their respective *isolaria*.

Farewell to the last Governor of Cyprus Sir Hugh Foot, centre, between President Makarios, centre right, and Vice-President Dr Fazil Kutchuk, centre left, on 16.8.1960
Photo: Press and Information Office

Political System – Administration

The Political Landscape

Parliamentary Political Parties

District Administration

Local Authorities

Council of Ministers

Photo: Press and Information Office

Political Landscape

Cyprus is an independent, sovereign Republic with a presidential system of government. A multi-party political landscape, with parties covering the whole spectrum of political ideologies, ensures the functioning of a free and democratic system.

Executive power is vested in the President of the Republic who is elected by universal suffrage for a five-year term. The executive power is exercised by the President through the eleven members of the Council of Ministers who are appointed by him. Ministerial portfolios include: defence; agriculture; natural resources and the environment; justice and public order; commerce, industry and tourism; foreign affairs; labour and social insurance; interior; finance; education and culture; communications and works; and health.

The President of the Republic of Cyprus is Tassos Papadopoulos, who was elected to office in February 2003, for a five-year term. The next

Cyprus House of Representatives

Photo: Press and Information Office

Ministry of Foreign Affairs

presidential elections will take place in February 2008.

Legislative power is exercised by the House of Representatives, which consists of one chamber with members elected for a five-year term. Fifty-six seats are held by Greek Cypriots and twenty-six are reserved for Turkish Cypriots. Since the withdrawal of the Turkish Cypriot members of the House in 1963, the Cyprus parliament has been functioning with only Greek Cypriot members.

The current electoral law provides for a simple proportional representation system. Each voter can choose a party or an independent candidate, without having the option of selecting candidates from different parties. Seats are distributed according to the electoral strength of each party.

In June 2001, the members of the House elected the General Secretary of AKEL, Demetris Christofias, President of the House of Representatives. He was re-elected President of the House in June 2006.

The administration of justice is exercised by the island's separate and independent judiciary through the following judicial institutions: the Supreme Court (the final appellate Court of the Republic), the Assize Court, the District Courts, the Military Court, the Rent Control Courts, the Industrial Disputes Court and Family Courts.

Independent Officers and Bodies

Certain officers and bodies are independent and do not come under any ministry. Such are the Attorney-General, the Auditor-General, the Governor of the Central Bank of Cyprus, the Ombudsman, the Public Service Commission and others. In recent years, a great number of new institutions with independent functions have been established due to the accession of Cyprus to the European Union.

Parliament in session

Parliamentary Political Parties

Progressive Party of Working People - AKEL

General Secretary: Demetris Christofias, President of the House of Representatives

A left-wing party, it was founded in 1941, based on Marxist-Leninist principles, taking into account current international political and economic developments. It supports an independent, demilitarised Cyprus and a federal solution to the internal aspect of the Cyprus problem. It places particular emphasis on rapprochement with the Turkish Cypriots.

Democratic Rally - DISY

President: Nicos Anastasiades, member of the House

A centre-right party, it was founded in 1976. It is a member of the European People's Party, Christian Democrat International, the European Democrat Union and the International Democrat Union. It supports a solution to the Cyprus problem on the basis of a bizonal, bicommunal federation.

Democratic Party-DIKO

President: Marios Karoyan, member of the House

A party of the centre, it was founded in 1976. It supports a settlement of the Cyprus problem based on UN resolutions. It has accepted the idea of federation.

Ministry of Finance

Movement of Social Democrats - EDEK

President: Yiannakis Omirou, member of the House

The party is the successor to the Socialist Party EDEK. It is a member of the European Socialist Party and Socialist International. It supports an independent and united Cyprus, within a federal system with a strong central government, and a settlement based on UN resolutions and the implementation of human rights for all its citizens.

European Party

President: Demetris Syllouris, member of the House

This centre party, established in July 2005, was a founding member of the European Democratic Party (EPD). It believes that the solution to the Cyprus problem should be compatible with the European acquis and based on UN resolutions as well as human rights. It is also in favour of closer EU involvement in the procedures toward a solution to the problem, in order to ensure, inter alia, that the European principle of abolishing artificial divisions is respected, and that both

Greek and Turkish Cypriots live together in a united island without ethnic or other segregation.

Ecological-Environmental Movement

General Secretary: George Perdikis, member of the House

Also calling itself the Cyprus Green Party. Founded in March 1996, the party is a member of the European Federation of Green Parties. It opposes any geographical division of the island or the people of Cyprus based on ethnic origin or religion. It is not in favour of any arms build-up.

Distribution of Seats in the House of Representatives (Following the 21 May 2006 parliamentary elections)

Party	Number of Seats
AKEL	18
DISY	18
DIKO	11
EDEK	5
EUROPEAN PARTY	3
ECOLOGISTS	1
	56

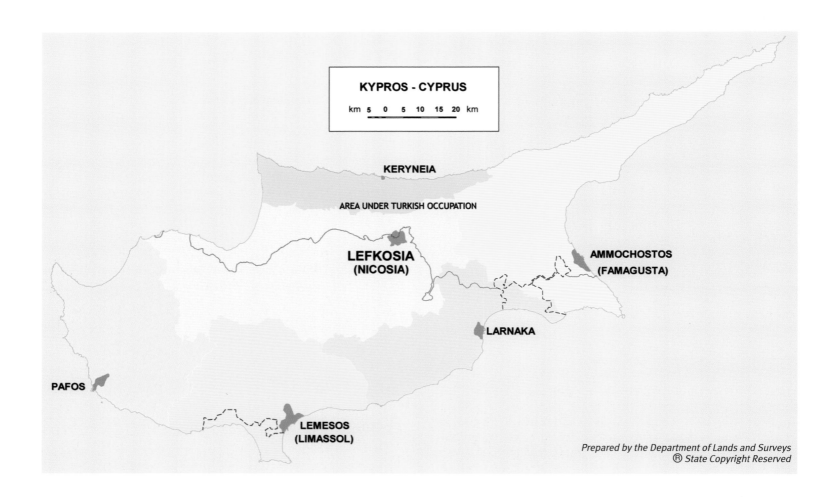

KYPROS - CYPRUS

km 5 0 5 10 15 20 km

KERYNEIA

AREA UNDER TURKISH OCCUPATION

LEFKOSIA
(NICOSIA)

AMMOCHOSTOS
(FAMAGUSTA)

LARNAKA

PAFOS

LEMESOS
(LIMASSOL)

Prepared by the Department of Lands and Surveys
Ⓡ State Copyright Reserved

District Administration

Cyprus is divided into six administrative districts. These are: Nicosia, Limassol, Pafos, Larnaka (in the government-controlled areas) and Famagusta and Keryneia (in the occupied areas). Each district is headed by a district officer. The district officer acts as the chief-coordinator of the activities of all ministries in the district. District officers are accountable to the Ministry of the Interior.

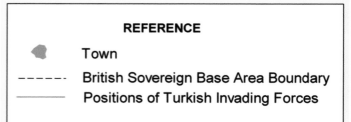

REFERENCE

Town

- - - - - British Sovereign Base Area Boundary

———— Positions of Turkish Invading Forces

Local Authorities

There are two types of local authorities in Cyprus, municipalities and communities, which are governed by separate laws. In principle, municipalities constitute the form of local government in urban and tourist centres, while communities constitute the local structure in rural areas.

Nicosia by night

Neighbourhood in the old part of Nicosia

Municipalities

Any community may become a municipality by local referendum, subject to the approval of the Council of Ministers, provided it has either a population of more than 5.000, or has the economic resources to function as a municipality.

Since the Turkish invasion of 1974 and the subsequent occupation of the northern part of Cyprus, nine municipalities, although still maintaining their legal status, have been temporarily relocated to the free areas.

Mayors are elected directly by the citizens, for a term of five years. The mayor is the executive authority of the municipality.

Municipal councils, which are the policy-making bodies of municipalities, are elected directly by the citizens for a term of five years, but separately from the mayor. The council appoints the members of the administrative committee. The latter's duties include the preparation of the municipality's budgets and annual financial statements, the provision of assistance and advice to the mayor in the execution of his duties, coordination of the work of other committees

Palm Trees Promenade, Larnaka

appointed by the council and the discharge of any other duties entrusted to it by the council or the mayor.

The main responsibilities of municipalities are the construction, maintenance and lighting of streets, the collection, disposal and treatment of waste, the protection and improvement of the environment and the good appearance of the municipal areas, the construction, development and maintenance of municipal gardens and parks and the protection of public health. The Municipal Council has the authority to promote, when fiscally feasible, a vast range of activities and events, including the arts, education, sports and social services. In addition to the Municipalities Law, there are several laws giving municipalities additional important powers.

The main sources of revenue of municipalities are municipal taxes, fees and duties including the following: professional tax, immovable property tax, hotel accommodation tax, permit and licence fees, fees for refuse collection, fines. They also receive state subsidies. Taxes, duties and fees represent the major source, while state grants and subsidies amount to only a small percentage of revenue. The central government, however, usually finances major infrastructure projects undertaken by the municipalities.

The Cyprus Flag

The Cyprus Flag and Emblem

The Cyprus Flag

The Flag

The Cyprus flag was defined in 1960 after Independence. The background of the flag is white, with a golden silhouette of the island in the middle, and two crossed olive branches below.

The international code numbers of the flag are:

Colour of ochre: PANTONE 1385
Colour of green: PANTONE 574

The colours were chosen for symbolic and practical reasons. The white background of the flag and the green olive branches symbolise peace and hope for reconciliation between the Greek and Turkish Cypriot communities. The silhouette of the island is golden/ochre for the sake of easier reproduction of what was originally intended to be a colour of copper, a metal that has been associated with Cyprus since antiquity.

Only the Constitution of the Republic of Cyprus has the authority to allow both state agencies and private citizens to fly national flags other than its own:

Part I

General Provisions

Article 4:

1. The Republic shall have its own flag of neutral design and colour, chosen jointly by the President and the Vice-President of the Republic
2. The authorities of the Republic and any public utility body created by or under the laws of the Republic shall fly the flag of the Republic and they shall have the right to fly on holidays together with the flags of the Republic both the Greek and the Turkish flag at the same time.
3. The Communal authorities and institutions shall have the right to fly on holidays together with flag of the Republic either the Greek or the Turkish flag at the same time.
4. Any citizen of the Republic or any body, corporate or unincorporate other than public, whose members are citizens of the Republic, shall have the right to fly on their premises the flag of the Republic or the Greek or the Turkish flag without any restriction.

The Cyprus Emblem

The Emblem

The colours of the Cyprus emblem are as follows: the outside frame is white, the crest of olive tree leaves is green (PANTONE 574), and the inside frame of the shield is golden-like ochre (PANTONE 1385). Inside the shield, the dove, the branch of olive tree in its mouth, and the year 1960 appear in white.

The olive branch and the dove symbolise peace and the year 1960 is the date of Cyprus' Independence.

Dairy products industry

Economy

Basic Characteristics

Tourism

Trade

Manufacturing and Industry

Agriculture

Water Management

Marine Resources

Merchant Shipping

Pharmaceuticals industry

Basic Characteristics

The economy of Cyprus is small, robust and fairly flexible that has shown itself able to adapt to rapidly changing circumstances. The economy is characterised by a very satisfactory rate of growth (the average annual rate of growth of GDP amounted to 5.1 percent, in real terms, over the period 1961-2006), full employment conditions and internal and external macroeconomic stability. As a result, Cyprus has achieved an enviable level of real convergence with advanced economies, with a per capita GDP in 2005, expressed in purchasing power standards, standing at around 89 percent of the EU25 average, according to the latest Eurostat figures and exceeds that of the rest of the new member states.

In brief, the basic characteristics of the Cyprus economy are the following:

- The dominant role of the private sector in the production process
- The small size of the domestic market

  The population in the Government-controlled areas was 854 300 in 2005, out of which 69.4 percent lived in urban areas and 30.6 percent in rural areas. The small size of the domestic market constitutes an adverse factor in the realisation of economies of scale and in the development of satisfactory intersectoral relationships.

- The small size of enterprises

  According to the Registration of Establishments, the size of enterprises remained very small, with 4,4 persons on average per unit in 2000, as compared to 4,3 persons in 1995. More than half of the total number of enterprises (58 percent) employed only one person. Micro enterprises, that is, enterprises employing less than ten persons, constituted 95 percent of the total, other small-size enterprises with ten to forty-nine employees constituted 4 percent and medium-size enterprises, with 50-249 employees, constituted only 0.7 percent of the total. There were only sixty-seven large enterprises, with a workforce exceeding 250 employees, representing 0.1 percent of the total number of enterprises. The small size of the business units hinders the exploitation of economies of scale and the adoption of advanced technologies and modern methods of management, production design and marketing.

- The small size of the labour force, given the small population base and certain quantitative and qualitative imbalances in the labour market

  The quantitative and qualitative imbalances are evident both at the sectoral and occupational levels and have been ameliorated by the employment of foreign labour. At the sectoral level, the imbalances are more evident in the sectors of hotels and restaurants, construction, agriculture and manufacturing, whereas at the occupational level, shortages are observed intechnical and low-skill occupations.

- The openness of the economy, with total imports and exports of goods and services accounting for 97.2 percent of GDP in 2006 as compared to an EU25 average of eighty percent

- The predominance and increasing importance of the services sectors, which accounted for 77.6 percent of GDP and 71 percent of total gainful employment in 2006.

  This development reflects the gradual restructuring of the Cypriot economy from an exporter of minerals and agricultural products, mainly copper, asbestos and citrus fruits in the period 1961-73 and an exporter of manufactured goods, mainly clothing and footwear, in the latter part of the 1970s and the early part of the 80s, to an international tourist, business and services centre during the 1980s, 1990s and the 2000s.

- Partial dependence on the tourism sector.

  During the past years, the total contribution of the tourism sector was contained to levels below 15 percent of GDP, as a result of the decrease of tourist arrivals and the per capita expenditure.

Accession to the Eurozone

Following Cyprus' accession to the EU, on 1 May 2004, the government of the Republic of Cyprus undertook the obligation to join the Economic and Monetary Union and to adopt the euro as soon as the necessary requirements were fulfilled. On 2 November 2005, the Council of Ministers determined 1 January 2008 as the target date for adoption of the euro in Cyprus. Thus, euro banknotes and coins will be the country's legal tender.

The euro banknotes are exactly the same in all euro countries. The euro coins have a side which is common for all euro countries and a national side which shows country-specific designs. The Cyprus euro coins depict – on their national side – themes which reflect the island's civilisation, history and wildlife.

The 1 and 2 euro coins depict a cross-shaped idol which dates back to the Chalcolithic period (3000 B.C.). It is a characteristic example of prehistoric art in Cyprus and presents the heritage and civilisation of a country with a history of over 10 000 years.

The 10, 20 and 50 cent coins depict the Keryneia ship, a replica of a fourth century B.C. Greek merchant ship. The wreckage of that ship was discovered on the seabed off the coastal town of Keryneia. Its depiction on the euro coins symbolises the importance of the sea as well as shipping and trade for Cyprus, throughout the island's history.

The 1, 2 and 5 cent coins depict the mouflon, which symbolises the island's rich wildlife. The mouflon is a unique spices of wild sheep endemic to Cyprus and is considered one of the natural treasures of the island.

Ayia Napa seaside resort

Photo: Cyprus Tourism Organisation

Tourism

The foundations of tourism in Cyprus were laid in the early sixties. Its progress was smooth and successful until the summer of the 1974 Turkish invasion. Then, all economic activity came to a standstill and the tourist sector suffered a devastating blow.

The destruction of the country's economy called for drastic measures, which would enable its quick reconstruction. The government decided that tourism was the tool to generate fast economic growth.

This task was achieved through the Cyprus Tourism Organisation (CTO), a semi-government organisation which comes under the Ministry of Commerce, Industry and Tourism, and which is responsible for the planning, promotion and marketing of tourism and the regulation and supervision of all tourist enterprises of the island.

The Cyprus Tourism Organisation was quick to respond to that challenge and successfully spearheaded the reconstruction effort. Soon enough, the island got back on the global tourist map, and tourism became the backbone and the main driving force behind the miraculous recovery of the Cypriot economy.

Coral Bay, Pafos

Photo: Cyprus Tourism Organisation

Post-1974 expansion has focused on the area of Ayia Napa, situated to the south of the occupied town of Famagusta, and the coastal towns of Larnaka, Limassol and Pafos. The effects of this transition have been most apparent on Ayia Napa itself. From a tiny village of a few hundred inhabitants clustered around a beautiful sixteenth-century Venetian monastery, the place has mushroomed into a sprawling conglomeration of holiday cottages, tourist shops, pubs, restaurants, hotels and discotheques. While this has marred the quaint charm of the former fishing village, it has made it a lively spot for young tourists and Cypriots alike. Along the coast from Ayia Napa are some of the most beautiful beaches found on the island, with their fine flour-like sand and turquoise waters.

The other large resort is that of Protaras on the eastern coast. Part of the Famagusta Bay area, Protaras is sheltered from the prevailing northeasterly winds and thus enjoys calmer seas. This makes it very popular with water-sport enthusiasts.

Efforts to facilitate the growth of tourism have been helped not only by nature but history as well. Sandy beaches, a warm sea and invariably reliable sunshine are a major attraction for tourists. But thousands of years of civilisation have also left a heritage of Greco-

One of the countless sandy beaches in Cyprus (Larnaka Bay)

Photo: Cyprus Tourism Organisation

Roman archaeological sites, mediaeval castles and Byzantine churches which tourists find equally irresistible. Hard work and the Cypriot temperament have also played a role. A time-honoured tradition of hospitality ('foreigner' and 'guest' are expressed by the same word in Greek) guarantees a warm welcome to visitors. "Well met in Cyprus" is a phrase which still echoes around the island. Little did Shakespeare, whose Othello originated the greeting, realise that his words would be such an apt depiction of Cypriot hospitality.

The major share of the tourist traffic to Cyprus originates from western, central and northern Europe. The United Kingdom remains the major source of tourist traffic, contributing almost 60 percent of the total tourist arrivals, followed by Germany, Greece, Russia, Sweden and Ireland. Other European countries, Israel and U.S.A. are also important contributors to tourist traffic to Cyprus.

Protaras Fig Tree Bay   Photo: Christos Violaris

Village of Kakopetria, Troodos mountains   Photo: Cyprus Tourism

Accommodation

Cyprus offers a wide variety of holiday accommodations ranging from modern, large and luxurious establishments to small and simple family-run operations. Holiday accommodation includes hotels, hotel apartments, tourist villages, tourist villas, camping sites, traditional houses, tourist apartments, furnished apartments, guesthouses and hotels without star. Accommodation in private houses is not available.

The modern tourist accommodation infrastructure in Cyprus is recognised as one of the strengths of the island's tourist product, mainly due to strict legislation governing the establishment and operation of hotels which demands high standards in accommodation facilities.

Agrotourism (Green Cyprus)

The development of agrotourism in Cyprus began in the early nineties and was promoted via a special incentives scheme administered by CTO to encourage the owners of traditional houses in the countryside to restore and convert them into tourist uses (accommodation establishments, tavernas, restaurants, cultural centres, handicraft centres, etc).

Currently, more than eighty four traditional houses in thirty-seven villages, with a total capacity of about 600 beds, have already been converted into accommodation establishments in accordance with the relevant regulations and received their classification and operation license from CTO. Still others are currently going through the above procedure.

Photo: Cyprus Tourism Organisation

Platres village, Troodos mountains

Photo: Press and Information Office

The owners of such traditional houses are assisted in their marketing efforts by the Cyprus Agrotourism Company, a non-profit association which was established in 1996 after a CTO initiative to encourage small property owners to become members in order to help them coordinate individual marketing efforts and incoming bookings. The Cyprus Agrotourism Company has set up a Central Reservations Office with a central reservations system and a website on the internet (www.agrotourism.com.cy), which allows visitors to that site to book online, with real-time confirmation. Furthermore, houses belonging to members of the Cyprus Agrotourism Company are featured in the Traditional Homes Guide, which is published in five languages and distributed free of charge through CTO Offices in Cyprus and abroad.

Since Cyprus' accession to the EU, there has been a new phase in the development of agrotourism. The whole of the Cypriot hinterland was declared a Target 2 area, and a new financial assistance scheme aimed at the development of small and medium-size enterprises related to agrotourism replaced the previous one.

This new, generous scheme is expected to contribute significantly toward the creation of other agrotourism infrastructure (such as handicraft and folk art centres, museums and small wineries) which will complement the accommodation offerings, and thus assist in the development of a well-rounded agrotourist product.

Trooditissa Monastery, in the Troodos mountains, where monks are known for producing excellent quality rosewater

Photo: Press and Information Office

Mountain Resorts

The undulating hillsides of the Troodos mountains are spotted with hundreds of tiny villages which offer a cool retreat from the hustle and bustle of the beaches, especially in summer. In winter the same mountains offer the option of an alpine-style holiday.

The highest point on Troodos is Mount Olympus, (1 952 metres), easily discernible from almost any place of the island. A little below it stands the village of Troodos. The summer seat of government during British rule, it now has a few hotels and restaurants, and an expanding ski area resort with four ski runs - two beginners' slopes, an intermediate and an advanced run on the north side. The skiing season lasts a couple of months a year, peaking in February.

Other favoured summer retreats in the mountains are the villages of Prodromos, Pedoulas and Platres. The latter is the most cosmopolitan of the mountain villages and was once a favourite summer home for the affluent from Limassol and Nicosia, not to mention the wealthy regular visitors from neighbouring countries who spent their summer there. Their sumptuous, stone-built holiday villas now line the narrow roads in the area. Today, however, many of these houses have been converted into guest houses for city dwellers during the summer months, particularly during the annual holiday in August. Apart from this period, peace and tranquility reign.

Nestling lower down in a deep valley amidst poplars, fruit trees and vines is the village of Kakopetria. The old part of the village which climbs the hillside from an unused mill has been declared an ancient monument and restored to its former glory of cobbled streets and old stone and adobe houses.

Cyprus' mountain villages are host to some of the most important examples of early Christian art. Part of the Byzantine Empire for

Traditional village coffee shop

Photo: Cyprus Tourism Organisation

almost eight hundred years, the island bore witness to one of the most creative periods in Christian church architecture and painting. Because of the island's remoteness, this heritage escaped the disastrous, religious conflicts of the time, especially destruction by the Iconoclasts. As a result, the chapels with their beautiful religious frescoes are living museums of Byzantine art.

In all, there are some five thousand churches and chapels in Cyprus, five hundred of them with vestiges of their original frescoes and hundreds more housing ancient icons. Many of the churches retain apse mosaics of the early Byzantine period—exceptional rare survivors of the Iconoclastic assault. Nine Cypriot churches containing especially fine examples of this church art were recently given the distinction of inclusion on UNESCO's world heritage list. These churches are: Asinou, Ayios Nikolaos tis Stegis, St John's Monastery (Lambadistis), Panayia tou Moutoulla, Archangelos at Pedoulas, Stavros at Pelendri, Panayia tou Araka at Lagoudera, Panayia tis Podhithou at Galata and Stavros tou Ayiasmati near Platanistasa.

Nature Trails

Cyprus offers a network of seventy two nature trails, which cover over 322 kilometres. These trails are located in areas of natural beauty such as the Troodos mountains, the Pafos and Adelphi Forests, the Cape Greco and Athalassa National Forest Parks, the Pitsilia area and the Marathasa Valley.

Trails within state forests are maintained by the Forestry Department, whereas trails elsewhere are maintained by local authorities. Trails

Cape Greco national forest park   **Photo: Department of Forests**

have been sign-posted in order to provide users with information on the local flora, fauna and geology.

In the last few years, several thematic trails were developed. These trails cover themes such as medieval bridges in the Pafos Forest, centenarian trees, traditional activities in villages of the hinterland and waterfalls.

The European long distance path E4 was extended to Cyprus following a proposal by the Greek Ramblers Association to the European Ramblers Association. The main partners in Cyprus are the Cyprus Tourism Organisation and the Forestry Department.

The Cyprus section of the E4 Path with a total length of 539 kilometres connects Larnaka and Pafos international airports. Along the route, it crosses the Troodos mountain range, Akamas peninsula and long stretches of Cypriot rural areas, along regions of enhanced natural beauty and areas of high ecological, historic, archaelogical, cultural and scientific value.

The European Blue Flag Campaign

The Blue Flag is an exclusive eco-label awarded to beaches that meet a number of criteria, including the quality of bathing water, environmental education and information and beach area management and safety. In 2006, a total of forty-nine beaches in Cyprus were awarded the European Blue Flag by the European Jury.

Limassol port

TRADE

Due to its small domestic market and open economy, Cyprus depends on, and considers access to, international markets of utmost importance. As a result, trade has always been essential to the island's economy and over the years contributed considerably to its growth. During 2005 exports accounted for about 9 percent of the country's GDP.

To keep abreast in the world and further enhance its economic and political development, Cyprus took a decisive step: in May 2004 it joined the EU. This bold decision has proved to be a defining moment that has already affected the country's international trade and fostered exports as a driving force in the economy.

During 2005, the first full year as a member in the EU, Cyprus experienced dynamic changes in the trade sector over the year 2004.

There was an increase in both exports and imports. Exports of domestic products increased by 8 percent, from CY£235 m. to CY£254 m., and re-exports by 48 percent, from CY£313 m. to CY£465 m. Total imports increased by 11 percent, from CY£2.679 m. to CY£2.967 m.

The main products exported were pharmaceuticals, citrus, halloumi cheese, fish and potatoes. Exports of manufactured products, which constitute 57 percent of domestic exports, increased from CY£132 m. to CY£136 m.

Exports of processed agricultural products increased to CY£42 m., representing 18 percent of the total. Domestic exports of raw agricultural products declined from CY£57 m. to CY£55 m., accounting for 22 percent of domestic exports. Exports of processed minerals experienced a decline from CY£5.5 m to CY£3.4 m. Exports of unprocessed minerals remained at about the same levels around CY£3.0 m., representing one percent of total domestic exports.

European Union countries, the biggest markets for Cyprus, absorbed 49 percent, or CY£126 m. of its domestic exports, with the United Kingdom, Greece and Germany leading the way. Near and Middle Eastern countries, the second biggest markets, absorbed about 13 percent of Cyprus' domestic exports. The major markets in this group are the United Arab Emirates, Iraq, Saudi Arabia, Lebanon and Jordan.

Imports of consumer goods and raw materials account for most of the total imports, 33 percent and 27 percent respectively. They are followed by fuels and lubricants (16 percent), transport equipment (13 percent), and capital goods (9 percent).

In 2005, European Union countries continued to be the biggest suppliers of goods to Cyprus providing 66 percent of the total imports, or goods valued at CY£1.954 m., with Greece, Italy, Germany, the United Kingdom, and the Netherlands being the major exporters to the island. Asian countries, the second most important group of suppliers, furnished Cyprus with goods valued at CY£334 m. or 11 percent of the total. The most important of these suppliers were China, Japan, Israel, South Korea, Thailand, Taiwan, Singapore and India.
(Note: For updates on figures and statistics please refer to the website of the Ministry of Finance at www.mof.gov.cy)

MANUFACTURING AND INDUSTRY

By 2005 the manufacturing sector accounted for 9.2 percent of the Gross Domestic Product and 10.5 percent of employment, with the export of manufactured goods in 2005 reaching CY£182 million. The most important sub-sectors in terms of value added are food and beverages, pharmaceutical and metal products, followed by other sub-sectors such as printing and publishing and chemical products.

The manufacturing industry in Cyprus is facing increasing

Photo: Press and Information Office

competition. At the root of the problem lie the structural weakness of the sector, the rising labour costs and low productivity. International competition is increasingly intensified mainly from two directions: On the one hand, the high-wage producers, who have combined design, quality and new forms of flexible production and on the other the low-wage mass producers of China and South-East Asia.

Faced with this situation the Government has reformulated government policy to facilitate technological upgrading of the industry. More specifically the Government has set the following priorities:

- To attract and develop high-tech industries
- To assist in the reconstruction of existing industries
- To improve productivity
- To attract foreign investment

Foreign capital can play a major role in these efforts, as it contributes substantially to the introduction of high technology and expertise. Cyprus' membership in the European Union provides small and medium-size Cypriot enterprises opportunities to participate in the various programmes concerning industrial technology, professional training, and product development, etc thus further enhancing the process of restructuring. Cyrpiot firms are presented with the challenge of penetrating the European market of 450 million consumers.

Photo: Press and Information Office

SMALL AND MEDIUM-SIZE ENTERPISES IN CYPRUS

The economy of Cyprus is dominated by small enterprises (SMEs). The Government has emphasised the need for a regulatory climate conducive to investment, innovation and entrepreneurship and has demonstrated its willingness to remove unnecessary procedures that impede the development of SMEs. This policy for SMEs is in line with that of the European Union.

INDUSTRIAL ESTATES AND FREE ZONES

The government has established twelve Industrial Estates across the island and one Free Zone in Larnaka. There are currently about 600 industrial enterprise units operating in the Industrial Estates and engaged in a wide spectrum of activities. The Government has allocated to these industrial enterprises appropriate land, varying in size according to the needs of each unit, on a long term lease base. The yearly lease rental depends on the location of the Industrial Estate and currently generates annual revenue of CY£2.000 000 per year.

AGRICULTURE

The broad agricultural sector plays a fundamental role in the Cyprus economy, with respect both to production of essential food items for domestic consumption and exports and also to employment of thousands of rural residents and the containment of the depopulation of villages.

During the period 1960-1974, the agricultural sector expanded rapidly, but in 1974 it was severely affected by the Turkish invasion and occupation. Turkish forces occupied an area which accounted for 46 percent of crop production and much higher percentages of citrus (79 percent), cereals (68 percent), tobacco (100 percent), carobs (86 percent) and green fodders (65 percent); the area also accounted for 45 percent of livestock production.

Despite the concentration of population in the less productive part of the island, it was possible through concerted efforts and heavy investment in land improvement and irrigation to reactivate the agricultural sector and to reach the pre-1974 production levels.

Photo: Andreas Andreou

Open-air market in Nicosia

The broad agricultural sector contributes about 3.6 percent to GDP and employs some 7.1 percent of the total economically active population. Agricultural exports (raw and processed) constitute some 30.7 percent of total domestic exports.

The two major sub-sectors of agriculture are crop and livestock production which contribute, at current prices, 48.7 percent and 42.7 percent respectively to the value added of the broad agricultural sector. The contribution of the other sub-sectors is as follows: ancillary production (milk and grape products processed on farm) about 4.7 percent, fishing 4.2 percent, forestry 0.6 percent and others 3.2 percent.

Harmonisation with the Common Agricultural Policy (CAP) of the European Union and implementation of the *acquis communautaire* in general will be the basic objective, as regards the agricultural sector, during the coming years.

Farmakas Dam

Photo: Conastantinos Charalambous

Photo: Press and Information Office

WATER MANAGEMENT

Throughout its long history, Cyprus has been confronted with the problem of water shortage. Having no rivers with perennial flow and highly variable precipitation, the country experiences frequent droughts. The mean annual precipitation, including snowfall, amounts to approximately 500 millimetres, whereas during the past thirty years (1973-2003) this amount fell to 480.

Until 1970, groundwater was the main source of water for both drinking and irrigation purposes. As a result, almost all aquifers were seriously depleted because of over-pumping, and seawater intrusion was observed in most of the coastal aquifers. At the same time, large quantities of surface water were lost through runoffs.

The water problem and its exacerbation over the years were recognised early enough by the relevant state authorities which, aided by international organisations, designed a long-term programme to combat the problem effectively.

After independence, attention was turned to the systematic study and construction of water development works, both for storage and recharge purposes. The first step involved a comprehensive survey of the island's water resources, followed by the implementation of a long-term plan for the construction of major development projects, which involved the construction of a large number of dams.

Today, the total storage capacity of the dams is about 307,5 million cubic metres of water, compared to 6 million in 1960, an impressive accomplishment when comparing Cyprus to other countries of the same size and development level.

Despite the remarkable progress in the sector, quantities of water available for human consumption and irrigation were not adequate. This was due to an increased demand for water, declining precipitation, and global climate changes and the greenhouse phenomenon.

To remedy the situation, desalination units were constructed aiming at rendering water supply for the major residential and tourist centres independent of rainfall.

Aquaculture

MARINE RESOURCES

Cyprus has developed activities in multidisciplinary fields concerning the sustainable use of marine resources, the development and sound management of fisheries and aquaculture, marine ecology, the protection of endangered species and habitats, physical and chemical oceanography and the prevention and combat of marine pollution.

Moreover, a contract for the installation of a Vessel Monitoring System (VMS) through satellite has been signed, and since 1 May 2004 all fishing vessels are equipped with a device to locate their exact fishing position, in order to control illegal fishing.

A fishing vessel register has been set up, and all fishing vessels will be registered in order to have a record of the fishing capacity of the Cyprus Fishing Fleet.

The Cyprus production of fish is about 3 750 tons valued at CYƟ13.8 million. Fish production is mainly derived from inshore fishery, trawl fishery, territorial and international waters and a purse seiner, as well as from aquaculture. The Cyprus fishing fleet consists of 500 fishing boats, 18 trawlers and 35 sword fishing vessels.

There are currently ten fishing shelters in operation at Paralimni, Ayia Triada, Ayia Napa, Potamos, Xylophagou, Ormideia, Larnaka, Ayios Georgios, Pomos and Pyrgos. Fishing vessels are also harboured at Latsi and in the ports of Pafos, Limassol and Larnaka.

A decision has also been made for the construction of an auction centre which with Cyprus joining the European Union is more than a necessity. The auction centre will include inland installations for the trade of fishery products as well as a port for the fishing vessels.

Limassol port

Photo: Christos Violaris

MERCHANT SHIPPING

The Cyprus Register of Ships has shown phenomenal growth in the last twenty years. In the early eighties, Cyprus ranked thirty-second on the list of leading maritime nations. It now ranks in tonnage terms as one of the ten largest in the world and the third largest fleet in the EU. In 2006, there were 1 845 vessels totaling 21 994 770 GT registered in the Cyprus Register of Ships.

Regarding the further development of Cyprus' merchant shipping and the enhancement of its international reputation as a maritime flag, the government has concluded cooperation agreements on merchant shipping with other countries. It also participates as a full member in the activities of all international organisations which are involved in shipping. Cyprus has also ratified several international conventions, which are in force globally, and is the first International Register that has voluntarily undergone the International Maritime Organisation (IMO) Member States Audit with full success. The Cyprus maritime

Photo: Press and Information Office

flag appears on the white side of the Paris and the Tokyo Memorandums of Understanding on Port State Control.

Cyprus is a leading third-party ship management centre. The island's location together with a unique package of advantages such as legal system, high level of professionalism in the legal and accounting sectors, excellent banking services, telecommunications and air links to all important destinations have enabled the country to play a prominent role in its success as an international business centre, including shipping-related activities.

Furthermore, the government has enacted legislation containing especially favourable provisions for shipping companies, including tax exemptions for income derived from the operation of ships, no tax on profits from the operation of Cyprus vessels or on dividends received from a ship-owning company, and no capital gains tax on the sale or transfer of a Cypriot vessel or of the shares of a ship-owning company. Cyprus has established maritime offices in Piraeus, London, New York, Rotterdam and Hamburg.

The political and economic contribution of merchant shipping is of great importance. Through shipping, Cyprus has distinguished itself by achieving remarkable international ranking and recognition far beyond its boundaries.

Cruise-liner leaving the port of Limassol

Ports

All port facilities of the island are under the jurisdiction of the Cyprus Ports Authority (CPA), a statutory body set up in 1973. It is practically the only investor in ports and carries out part of the port operations, mainly pilotage, cranage and store keeping.

However, the bulk of activity, stevedoring and shore operations are in the hands of the private sector. This has enabled Cyprus ports to reach high levels of productivity and the private sector to develop an integrated package of services to cater to customer needs. These services extend beyond the boundaries of ports and even overseas, to cover logistical support, warehousing, distribution and supplying services to a wide international region.

Being a small island state, Cyprus relies entirely on ports for its connection to other countries as far as cargo movement is concerned. In addition, its ports play a major role in the movement of passengers, mostly cruise passengers, thereby enhancing the very important tourist sector. Indeed, the island is a well-established cruise hub in the Eastern Mediterranean. Until recently, Cyprus ports were important transhipment centres in the region, offering cost-effective services to international trade and making a substantial contribution to the economy of the country. With accession, Cyprus has become the EU's southeastern outpost.

Sea-borne traffic is serviced in Cyprus by a modern and highly integrated national port system, composed of the multipurpose ports of Limassol and Larnaka, the industrial port of Vassiliko and four specialised oil terminals at Larnaka, Dekeleia, Moni and Vassiliko.

Limassol port serves the country's overseas trade and sea-borne passenger traffic and acts as a transhipment centre for the region. With a quay length of 2 030 metres and dredged depth to fourteen metres, the port is equipped with post-panamax cranes to serve even fourth-generation container vessels. It offers the full complement of services required during a ship's call to port, including ship repair, container repair, bunkering, ship-handling, etc.

Larnaka port, with a quay length of 666 metres and dredged depth to twelve metres, serves some specialised trade and is scheduled for redevelopment into a specialised state-of-the-art passenger/leisure port.

The ports of Famagusta, Keryneia, Karavostassi and Xeros are in the area occupied by Turkish troops since 1974 and have been declared by the government of the Republic of Cyprus closed to shipping and navigation and as prohibited ports of entry and exit.

Traditional wine making

Wine Industry

According to tradition, Cypriots are the world's oldest winemakers (some findings establish the beginning at around 2000 B.C.). Faithful to this tradition, they now produce more wine per person than any other country in the world. Paradoxically, however, Cypriots also have one of the lowest per capita wine consumption rates in Europe. This means that the island's wine industry depends heavily on foreign markets for its products.

Wine has been part of Cyprus' history from the beginning. Where history fades into mythology, we find Bacchus and his friends enjoying a glass (or more) of Cyprus wine, and worshippers of Aphrodite celebrated with Cyprus' *nama*, said to be the oldest known wine in history. There was praise for Cyprus' wines in Homer, too, while in early Greek texts the island is referred to as *evinos* (of good wine).

The local dessert wine known as *Commandaria* is generally acknowledged as the oldest named wine in the world. It has been enjoyed and praised through the ages. Mark Antony, Shakespeare informs us, gave Cyprus to Cleopatra with the words: "your sweetness my love is equal to Cyprus nama." Among its fans was also King Philippe of France, who in the thirteenth century called it the "Apostle of Wines." And in the twelfth century, Richard the Lionheart was equally complimentary: "I must return to Cyprus, if only to taste this wine again," he is reported to have said on his departure.

Traditionally, Cyprus has had two main strains of grapevines: the *mavro* (red), which is the oldest in the world and unique to Cyprus, and the *xynisteri* (white). They produce full-bodied and, for some palates, rather strong products. This is why, since

Grape picking
Photo: Christos Violaris

Winery cellar
Photo: Press and Information Office

independence, Cyprus winemakers, in partnership with the government, have been experimenting with different European strains. Of the many tried, only a few have been found suitable to local conditions. Cultivation of these strains has been encouraged in order to produce lighter wines, of lower alcoholic content, and more suitable to the European palate. This process of adaptation is the reverse of that which took place in past centuries, when cuttings from Cyprus vines were transported by the Crusaders and other medieval travelers to Europe, where they won both fame and glory. Among the end products from such cuttings are Champagne, Madeira, Marsala and the Hungarian Tokay.

Since independence, wine has been a major foreign currency earner, and the introduction of new grape varieties is helping to further promote the industry. Europe is the major market for Cyprus' wines, with Germany absorbing some 1.000 000 litres in 2004. Other major markets include Britain, France and Russia. More recently, trade missions have intensified their efforts in the potentially huge markets of the U.S.A. and Japan. In 2004 some 108 516 tons of grapes were produced, mainly in the Limassol and Pafos Districts.

Production methods in Cyprus' wineries are among the most advanced in the world, and large sums are invested to ensure consistent quality. Tradition, however, still plays an

Photo: Cyprus Tourism Organisation

important role, not least in the production of *Commandaria*. This dessert wine is made from the sweet grapes of a small area on the southern slopes of the Troodos mountains, which includes the thirteen Commandaria villages. Here the grapes are spread out to dry in the sun for ten to fifteen days before they are pressed. The run-off juice is collected for fermentation in tanks, although in some places earthen jars are still used.

A view of a rural house courtyard through the portico

Photo: Department of Town Planning and Housing

Culture

Traditional Architecture

Theatre

Museums

Handicrafts

Sports

Cinema

Mountain settlement
Photo: Department of Town Planning and Housing

Traditional Architecture

Cyprus' rich history, from the dawn of human civilisation to the end of the Middle Ages, is documented by significant monuments. But alongside the ancient ruins and the Byzantine churches lies the anonymous vernacular architecture, which forms the built environment of our historic settlements. The traditional buildings, constructed to shelter the life and aspirations of ordinary people, encapsulate the material expression, the living testimony of the culture, the beliefs and the social, political and economic circumstances of our ancestors.

The form and organisation of settlements and the vernacular buildings that create them depend on the topography of the land, the climatic conditions, the available materials and their properties, but also on socio-economic factors. The villages seem to organically grow into the landscape, whether that is part of steep mountains, rounded hills or plains, forming a remarkable unity of the natural and manmade environments. Settlements were compact, densely built, with narrow, earthen or stone-paved streets uniting the individual dwellings and tracing the way to the agricultural land in the outskirts. The church was the most important part of the historic core, a gathering place for the social and economic activity of the inhabitants. Other public spaces were rare, usually developed alongside the main road leading to the settlement.

Life in the iliakos *(sun-room)*

Photo: Department of Town Planning and Housing

The Rural House

The rural house was built by the local dwellers without following a set plan, but according to the needs of the family. The organisation of the house reflected the introverted nature of the community. The closed inner courtyard was the heart of the house, a main living and working space for both people and animals. Surrounded by high walls, it was an inherent and necessary component of the dwelling space and provided access to the different parts of the house. This was usually composed of two or three *makrinaria* (narrow long rooms), cellars and/or *dichora* (double space rooms) which were always positioned against the edges of the plot, either in a linear or in an L-shape formation. Access to the courtyard from the house was achieved via a

Palati

Photo: Department of Town Planning and Housing

courtyard door that led straight to it, or through a semi-opened arched portico. The rooms were rarely linked to each other and had doors usually only facing the courtyard. The *dichoro* was the most important internal space of the house. It had multiple functions; it served as living and sleeping room, reception space, but could also house the animals. It was formed by doubling the width of a *makrinari* by replacing the wall in between with a wooden beam spanning the whole length of the room, or by inserting a stone arch in the place of the dividing wall. When the arch was used, this room was called *palati* (palace).

The *iliakos* (sun-room) was another important feature of the traditional house. It was a semi-covered space, open on one side toward the courtyard facing the sun, by one or more consecutive arches or beams on poles, according to its length. It also provided access to the adjacent rooms of the house. In many cases the *iliakos* was repeated on the upper floor. These were the most interesting morphological features of the whole composition of the dwelling.

A second floor was built usually when the plot was small and did not allow for ground floor extensions. Access to the second floor rooms was always via an external stone or wooden staircase located in the

House in rural environment

House in rural environment   Photo: Department of Town Planning and Housing

Mountain village   Photo: Department of Town Planning and Housing

courtyard against the front elevation of the main house and usually ending in a small covered wooden balcony. The doors and windows were small and few and proportioned according to the structural qualities of the building materials. Openings toward the street were scant, usually with only a front door and an *arsera* (a small window)

high above it for ventilation. The houses were always positioned toward the south or the east to absorb as much sunlight as possible.

On higher elevations on the mountains, the topography of the land limited the space available for housing. In this case a courtyard was rare and the buildings seem to be clambered on several levels on the steep slope. The different levels of the houses were accessed straight from the streets at different elevations. There was often an *iliakos*, this time on the highest level of the house, forming a kind of covered verandah.

The Urban House

The transition from the rural to the urban type of dwelling began toward the end of the nineteenth and the beginning of the twentieth century, almost coinciding with the end of the Ottoman era. It also coincided with the emergence of the Cypriot middle class, the result of socio-economic restructuring that brought with it a new perception of social and economic practices. The forms of the buildings consequently began to alter. With the new practices, the main rooms of the dwelling were defined, organised and all built together, at the same time. The middle-class owner began to create his own dwelling space, suited to his own specific needs, but still borrowed from the basic layout of the rural dwelling (which had by then become unsuited to his lifestyle). For some time, various areas, such as the kitchen, washroom and laundry room, remained in separate units from the main building due to their diminished importance as spaces for social functions. The location of the main house at the far end of the building plot became outmoded. The new urban type of dwelling, projected as one finite unit, needed to be displayed so that it could acquire social status. It was gradually brought forward toward the front of the building plot, bordering the street. The new style, dictated by modernisation, was the neoclassical style, whose morphological elements adorned city mansions but also influenced the humble buildings of the period, in both the urban and rural environment.

The individual rooms in a house were organised along a principle which was to become the nucleus for each urban housing unit. The central hallway or *iliakos* served as an entry space from the street, while one or two rooms (*makrinaria*) were located symmetrically on either side of it. If the width of the plot allowed, one of these *makrinaria* would become a *dichoro* by the use of an arch. Originally, the *iliakos* itself used to have an open arch toward the courtyard in the back which later was closed off with a door. Despite small changes, the *iliakos*, remained the main room of the house.

Later, the strict symmetry governing the layout of the house became more elastic. Serving as a central hallway, the *iliakos* continued to

Mountain village

Photo: Department of Town Planning and Housing

Urban house

Urban house

have the same ample proportions, but one of the side rooms became wider to accommodate important social functions and evolved into the salon. Other rooms became smaller. The final phase in the evolution of the urban dwelling was completed when the house included all its necessary spaces under one roof and became one individual free-standing unit, situated within an urban fabric of similar units. Inside the dwelling, the tripartite organisation of rooms in the layout continued to persist, but over time became subject to numerous alterations with a noticeable break-away from symmetry. One end of the *iliakos* could be separated down the middle with glazing, while often a verandah appeared in place of the *iliakos* at the back of the house. Despite variations, the whole building was gathered under a four-pitched tiled roof.

In the plan of the symmetrical house, balance was also reflected in its facade, with the front door placed at the center, flanked by a window on either side. In cases where the building was moved back from the street, a covered portico shaded the front entry. This was achieved by taking space from the front of the original *iliakos*. On other occasions a covered porch was added along the whole front of the house. Windows appeared on the side elevations of these free-standing houses, and the side elevations themselves acquired compositional importance.

Traditional Architecture today

With the introduction of new technology, the industrialised, easy-to-use new materials and the modern way of life, traditional architecture was inevitably abandoned. Contemporary architecture and techniques replaced or altered the historic building stock to a great extent. After a long period of indifference during which vernacular architecture was synonymous with rural misery, traditional architecture is once again appreciated for its cultural heritage value. Both rural and urban historic settlements enjoy a growing interest for their rehabilitation and revitalisation. The government supports this trend by providing generous financial and other incentives for restoration and rehabilitation projects and by organising events aiming at sensitising the public on the value of traditional architecture.

Theatre

Theatre in Cyprus has flourished since antiquity. The ancient theatres of Kourion, Pafos, Salamis(*) and Soli(*) testify to that.

The most important year in the modern history of Cyprus is 1878, when the island passed from the hands of the Ottoman Empire to the hands of Great Britain.

The fact that Cyprus was under British rule and very much oriented towards Hellenism contributed most significantly to the development of theatre on the island. Furthermore, the island was fortunate enough to be on the long theatre sea-route which began in Constantinople or Smyrna and stopped in Cyprus before reaching their destination in Egypt and the Greek communities of Palestine.

As a result, Cyprus provided fertile ground for action to all Greek visitors, even those of dubious quality. This was also true for Greek theatre companies, which to a large extent shouldered the burden of the theatrical life of the island from 1878 to 1940, with shows lasting several months. These companies gave performances mainly in towns but frequently in villages, too. Of greatest importance was the continuous presence of Greek theatre companies. In fact, local amateur theatre as well as Cypriot drama followed closely the model of Greek centres.

From the early twentieth century until 1940, except during World War I, Greek theatre companies of higher or lower standard, some totally insignificant, kept visiting the island. These theatre companies offered a wide repertoire: classical Greek and foreign nineteenth-century plays, Shakespeare and Molière, romantic comedies and romances, melodramas, patriotic plays, revues, etc.

Local theatre began on an amateur level and soon went through a renaissance. Apart from school drama, which was devoted exclusively to ancient plays, amateur theatres were run by various associations of political or social orientation which used theatre in order to promote their agendas, or by some other clubs whose main object of activity was the theatre. So, when the island was in the grips of the

The Papadopoulos Theatre, built in 1899

Agamemnon *by Aeschylus, Main Stage, Cyprus Theatre Organisation, 1971-72*

so-called Ecclesiastical Dispute[2], there were two associations: *I Agapi tou Laou* (Love of the People) representing Cypriots who took an intransigent stance on the Cyprus problem; and *Kypriakos Syndesmos* (Cypriot Association) whose members adopted a conciliatory position toward the British. These two entities had a very intense theatrical activity.

After 1920 and under the influence of new socio-political ideas, namely the Russian October Revolution, Cyprus saw the establishment of workers' unions, especially in Limassol and Nicosia, which were dedicated to the theatre or, rather, whose interests were served by the theatre. Consequently, during the 1920s Panergatikon (All workers) and soon thereafter the Shoemakers,' Barbers' and

Printers' unions developed an intense theatrical activity, usually staging plays depicting the oppression of the poor by the rich. This led to the establishment of a kind of primitive workers' theatre. At the same time, a number of artistic associations became active, especially in Limassol, usually presenting revues written by their members. There was such a frenzy for revues that in 1936 the policemen of each town staged their own productions in their efforts

[2] *The dispute between the two Bishops of Cyprus, Kyrillos of Kition and Kyrillos of Keryneia, both candidates for the throne of the Archbishop, in 1900. The struggle, whose origins were rooted in the desire for a more assertive national leadership, dragged on for a decade.*

Mother Courage and her Children
*by Bertolt Brecht, Main Stage, Cyprus
Theatre Organisation, 1977-78*
Photo: Cyprus Theatre Organisation

Euripides' Iketides, *ancient Kourion theatre, Cyprus Theatre Organisation, 1984*

to bridge the gap between the police force and the public. The judges and lawyers of Limassol did exactly the same in 1938!

The pioneers of this interesting activity, from the beginning to the end of British rule, were a number of Cypriot actors with relative experience, but mainly Greek actors, not of particularly high caliber, who for various reasons were left stranded on the island. These people were the driving force behind the theatrical activity on the island and, in a sense, were instrumental in preparing the ground for the professional theatre that was to follow.

During World War II (1940-45), with Greece under German occupation, Greek theatre companies stopped coming to the island. At the same time Greek cinema was nonexistent. This led to the development of local professional theatre companies, the most important being the Neon Lyrikon and the Nicosia Artists Union that

Spanos and the Forty Dragons, *Children's Stage, Cyprus Theatre Organisation, 1997*

staged revues as well as Greek and Viennese operettas with great success. The last year of the war saw the emergence of the first and most serious prose theatre company in Cyprus called Prometheas.

From 1945 to 1955 there was another mass wave of Greek theatre companies arriving on the island. It was a time when Greece faced very serious problems (the aftermath of the German occupation, the civil war and the ensuing famine), and those working in the theatre were forced to search for work in the Greek Diaspora communities. As a result, this intense activity by a great number of leading Greek names considerably hindered efforts toward the expansion of Cypriot theatre. The Cyprus Theatre, a company that emerged in 1950 and kept local professional theatre alive, was the exception.

Euripides' Troades, *Cyprus Theatre Organisation, 2003*

Photo: Christakis Avraamides

So, since under British rule (1878-1960) there was not a single piece of legislation governing the development of arts, it was Greek and Cypriot private individuals as well as the artistic and mainly workers' associations and unions that kept local theatre activity alive.

With Independence came dramatic changes. During the first year of the nascent republic, a theatre organisation known as OTHAC (Cyprus Theatre Development Organisation) was established, funded by the governments of Cyprus and Greece. OTHAC attempted to work on the basis of the rules of theatrical praxis and succeeded for several years, before it deteriorated and fell into disrepute by limiting its repertoire to farce.

The Other Half of the Sky *by Evridiki Perikleous, Cyprus Theatre Organisation, 2003*

Photo: Christakis Avraamides

In 1969, the Cyprus Broadcasting Corporation, then the only television station on the island, set up an arts theatre which gave performances of unprecedented caliber which they also broadcasted for Cypriot as well as Greek audiences. Unfortunately, this theatre was dissolved in 1971. In the same year, however, the Cyprus Theatre Organisation (THOC) was founded as a semi-governmental entity, whose goal was not only to create a theatre company but also to promote theatrical arts in Cyprus and create cultural links with other countries. The creation of THOC was the first serious attempt made by the government to create a state theatre.

THOC aspires to base its work primarily on the long tradition of theatre in Cyprus, a tradition closely interwoven with the principles of democracy, and to provide culture and entertainment to the citizens of the island. The vision of THOC for the future is now becoming all the more meaningful and important in order to ensure that Cyprus will be in a position to contribute in a qualitative way to European and worldwide culture and civilisation-a contribution that promotes communication among peoples through art and the presence of all arts in theatre.

THOC employs twenty-three actors on a regular basis and works with a group of internationally acclaimed stage directors, designers, composers and choreographers. It also employs actors on short-term contracts.

At present THOC operates four Stages: the Main Stage, the New Stage, the Experimental Stage and the Children's Stage. In thirty-three years of operation, the organisation has staged over three hundred plays, varying greatly in subject matter, dramatic genre, language, approach and philosophy:

- Main Stage: It is geared toward large-scale productions of classic and modern plays, as well as ancient drama.

- New Stage: Established in 1994, it promotes plays with small casts that are performed in smaller spaces for a more intimate interaction between stage and audience.

- Experimental Stage: It aims at developing research and promoting new forms of theatre.

- Children's Stage: It stages plays by playwrights from Cyprus, Greece and other countries, as well as productions of Shadow Theatre.

The organisation has toured abroad extensively, giving performances in the United Kingdom, Egypt, Germany, Bulgaria, Russia, Greece, the U.S.A., Poland, China and Denmark. Since 1980 THOC has taken part in the annual Epidaurus Festival in Greece, with plays from the ancient Greek drama repertoire.

Cyprus Theatre Museum

With a view to presenting a comprehensive overview of the history of theatre in Cyprus, THOC and the Municipality of Limassol have founded the Museum of the History of Cyprus Theatre. Original items being collected will be exhibited in the museum's various rooms. The museum also plans to house a theatre archive with access to researchers, students and theatre-enthusiasts. Aiming at attracting audiences of all ages, the museum will also organise in-house activities and events related to theatre and theatre practice.

Amateur Theatre

The Cyprus Theatre Organisation attaches particular importance to the development of amateur theatre, which is perhaps the purest expression of interest in theatre. A decision by any club or association to engage itself in the area of theatre is always welcomed, since it leads to new quests for creativity and quality performances.

As further incentive to groups that can demonstrate their involvement in the field of amateur theatre, the Cyprus Theatre Organisation offers the following:

- Inclusion in THOC's register of amateur theatre groups and dispatch of information regarding amateur theatre.

- Dispatch of a bi-monthly bulletin and complimentary tickets to THOC's performances.

- Organisation of the Pancyprian Festival of Amateur Theatre, in which groups can take part with performances given at venues of

Factory Girls, *Limassol Theatrical Development Company (ETHAL), 2003*

Photo: Christakis Avraamides

their choice. The best performance of the Festival goes on to represent Cyprus at the "Meeting of Amateur Groups of the Aegean," which takes place every autumn on an Aegean island. Each participating group receives a symbolic grant.

- Assistance in the selection of plays.

- Help and advice to amateur (and school theatre groups) by an actor/director employed by THOC.

- Contact data with other amateur groups based in Cyprus or Greece, with a view to promoting exchange programmes.

- Organisation of training seminars.

The Pierides Foundation Museum in Larnaka

Museums

The various museums exhibit ceramics, sculpture, metal objects, jewellery, tombs, inscriptions as well as objects of traditional arts and crafts, all of which witness different stages in the course of human presence on the island. The museums participate in many exhibitions around the world by lending objects relevant to the theme of the exhibition. The archaeology of Cyprus has enjoyed great attention by scholars who visit the island to study its monuments and antiquities. Numerous exhibitions and symposia/conferences related to the archaeology of Cyprus are organised every year abroad or in Cyprus.

The largest museum is the Cyprus Museum in Nicosia, while each district has its own museum; various smaller local or thematic museums were established at Kourion, (Episkopi), Kouklia

The Cyprus Museum, Nicosia

The House of Hadjigeorgakis Kornesios in Nicosia,
Europa Nostra Award, 1988

(Palaepafos) Maa-Palaeokastro and Marion-Arsinoe at Polis tis Chrysochous.

The Cyprus Medieval Museum is housed in the Castle of Limassol, while folk art museums were founded in Nicosia and Limassol and other smaller folk art museums at Fikardou, Yeroskipou and Pano Lefkara (Museum of Traditional Embroidery and Silversmithing). The House of Hadjigeorgakis Kornesios, the most important eighteenth century building in Nicosia, was restored to house a small ethnological collection, a project which received a Europa Nostra award in 1988.

Other museums include the Leventis Municipal Museum in Nicosia with exhibits that display life in the capital from ancient times to the present, the National Struggle Museum with memorabilia of the 1955-59 liberation struggle, the Museum of the History of the Cyprus Coinage (Nicosia), the Museum of Palaeontology and Marine Life of George Tornaritis and the Demetris Pierides Foundation in Larnaka with a unique collection of fossils, and the Pierides Foundation (Archaeological) Museum with a remarkable private collection.

Folk art museum
at the village of Fikardou
Photo: Press and Information Office

Handicrafts

Today more and more countries associate folk art with handicraft, that is, contemporary handicraft that people create based on the folk art of the country.

Contacts with neighbouring peoples and the presence of successive conquerors introduced elements that contributed to the formation of a different kind of folk art and handicraft in Cyprus. However, like in other eras, the island's art absorbed foreign elements but preserved its traditional character.

Photo: Press and Information Offic

Skilled craftsmen were greatly respected. Their craft, considered a family tradition, was passed down to their children. Trade in handicraft products was carried out mainly in towns. The biggest and best-known market was the famous Women's Bazaar in Nicosia held every Friday. Women from all over Cyprus would come to sell their wares, such as homespun and home-woven silks and cottons.

The main characteristic of Cypriot folk art is its geometrical, severe design. However, there is no lack of more freely patterned motifs from the plant and animal kingdoms, or of Hellenic and symbolic themes.

One of the main reasons why all the branches of folk art and handicraft were developed in Cyprus is the abundance of raw materials such as cotton, flax, silk, and wool for weaving and embroidery, pinewood and walnut trees for woodwork, clay for pottery and cane and wheat stems for basket weaving.

One of Cyprus' largest losses due to the 1974 Turkish invasion was the destruction of handicraft culture in the areas which are now occupied. Consequently, private as well as public collections which are in the free areas of the island have great importance. Especially rich in excellent items of folk art is the Ethnographic Museum which is housed in the former archbishopric in Nicosia.

Basket-weaving, Cyprus Handicraft Centre

Local craftsmanship includes colourful homespun linen, thatched chairs, painted gourds, silverware, pottery and intricate crochet. Although the occasional blacksmith and candlemaker can still be found in the narrow streets of Nicosia, and a potter or chairmaker can still do brisk business in the mountain village of Phini, in Cyprus, as in the rest of the world, mechanisation has taken its toll on traditional crafts.

Nevertheless, craftsmanship is far from extinct. The Cyprus Handicraft Service has expended great efforts to ensure that local craftwork enthusiasts would not have to resort to museums of popular art for a glimpse of traditional skills. Under a project launched in 1975, the service has given lessons in embroidery in rural centres and refugee settlements throughout the island. Experts have also delved deep into the past to rediscover traditional crafts. They have had much to consider: terracotta from Kornos, weaving from the Karpassia peninsula, gold and silver workmanship, carved wooden chests and lace form Athienou and Lefkara, and baskets and chairs from various regions. These have all been researched in detail, photographed, catalogued and reproduced in order to revive forgotten ideas on design and production.

The Handicraft Centre has also been established in Nicosia to act as a showpiece for the Handicraft Service and provide training. At the same time, incentives have been provided to village communities to

Pottery decoration, Cyprus Handicraft Centre

Photo: Press and Information Office

Cypriot silverwork

build up cottage industries. Especially successful has been the revival of lace in Athienou, Kornos and Kilani, and pottery in Kornos, Phini and Ayios Dimitrios.

The Handicraft Centre has become an important tourist attraction in its own right, providing quality products and training facilities. Experimental workshops are conducted in the fields of embroidery, weaving, tapestry, woodwork, pottery, metal works and general handicrafts, leather works and garment making. In these workshops, innovative samples are created under the supervision of qualified personnel. In addition, there are archives, an exhibition hall and a shop where the objects made at the Handicraft Centre and on a private basis are sold.

Apart from the Handicraft Centre there are also centres with shops in all the towns of the free areas as well as production units in houses and workshops in various villages.

Copper tradition since antiquity

Making lefkaritika

Lefkara Lace

Lefkara lace, perhaps the best known Cypriot traditional embroidery, enjoys a worldwide reputation. It has evolved though the ages, having undergone changes brought about by the history of the island. By studying its technique, motifs, local names, raw materials and designs, one can find traces of the past which enable one to discover the history and identity of the island.

Lefkara lace derives its name from the village of Lefkara, where the most difficult and complex designs are made. Lefkara lace is also made in the villages of Kato Drys, Ora, Skarinou, Athienou and

Example of Cypriot lace Photo: Cyprus Handicraft Centre

Four generations of women from the village of Lefkara engaged in lace making and embroidery, a family tradition Photo: Press and Information Office

Kornos. *Lefkaritika*, as the lacework is known, originated from the local white embroidery called *asproploumia*, which women throughout Cyprus made as part of their dowry. The all-white embroidery consisted of geometric patterns in satin stitch, combined with simple drawn-thread-work. Then, in medieval times the village of Lefkara became the favourite summer resort of the ruling Venetian families. Venetian ladies took their own embroidery there to while away the long, hot summer hours, and their designs influenced those of the local women, whose descendants produce today's lefkaritika.

Women do the needlework at home, and are often seen sitting in small groups, in doorways or courtyards, bent over their fine work. Patience and skill are very much required, as a single item may take months to complete.

Originally, the lace was embroidered on handmade cotton material, using cotton thread. This was later replaced by linen. Local silk production also permitted the introduction of silk lace material into the design.

Nowadays, Lefkara lace is made on linen material imported from various countries with mercerised cotton threads in white, natural colour or beige. The range of stitches and patterns of Lefkara embroidery is wide. Some derive from Venetian times, other motifs are pre-Venetian, still others are said to have been taken from the cave drawings of Ayios Neophytos, the twelfth-century Cypriot hermit.

Lefkara lace is made by counting the threads of the fabric. This is why most shapes are strictly geometrical. The embroidery consists of: (1) the designs which are embroidered over the cloth by using the satin stitch; and (2) the cut and drawn designs which are made after cutting and drawing specific threads of the fabric.

Most designs have names describing objects from everyday life. For the satin stitch designs, there are names such as lanterns, crosses, forks, snails and daisies, and for the cut and drawn designs names, such as basket-like, eye-like and flea-like.

An important feature of the Lefkara lace is "the river." This is a cut and drawn design with a zigzag shape. It runs parallel to the outside edges of the fabric. Its arches enclose triangular areas that are filled in with a variety of designs.

Also characteristic of the Lefkara lace are the designs made along the edges of the fabric. These are the *tsimbi, closi* and *tsimbocloso*. A

Tray cloth

Photo: Cyprus Handicraft Centre

Lefkara white embroidery design **Photo: Cyprus Handicraft Centre**

Lefkara white embroidery **Photo: Cyprus Handicraft Centre**

Lace from Lefkara, nineteeth century **Photo: Cyprus Folk Art Museum**

design which is no longer made is a kind of coarse lace, made by using the bobbin-lace technique common in Europe.

Lefkara lace is used mainly for tablecloths, napkins, tray-cloths and curtains. In the past it decorated the various parts of the four-poster bed, i.e., hangings, sheets, pillowcases, bedcovers and side and top curtains.

All these formed part of a girl's dowry, which was necessary for her future life. It was a form of artistic expression for young women that proved their skill and talent. In addition, it was a challenge which often resulted in the creation of masterpieces of art and craftsmanship.

Woven runner with phyti *designs*   Photo: Cyprus Handicraft Centre

Phyti Weaving

The origins of *Phyti weaving* are lost. It has evolved through time, having undergone changes brought about by the history of the island. Geometric patterns similar to motifs used in *Phyti weaving* were used since ancient times, as can be seen from pottery of the Geometric period.

Weaving was highly developed during Byzantine times and during the Venetian and Lusignan dynasties. In those days, Cypriot valuable silk and woolen fabrics were sought after for their high quality and exported in great quantities to Europe.

Bed cover with phyti *designs*   Photo: Cyprus Handicraft Centre

Phyti is the most important type of Cypriot weaving. Its main features are the colourful, geometric textured designs or ploumia, as they are called by the weavers, which are made on natural coloured cotton cloth.

The *ploumia* have mainly strong colours: blue, red, green, orange and yellow. They are made while weaving by using thick coloured threads or *fytilia* which are placed by the weaver among the warp threads.

Phyti weaving was mostly made into rectangular napkins, bed-covers and tablecloths. The most dominant shape of the design is the rhomb, which is made parallel to the narrow sides of the fabric. The designs usually come from items used in everyday life such as the black-eye design, or the teacher's shoe and carpet design. These wide designs are separated by parallel rows of narrow designs such as the little arch and fish-bone design. Toward the centre of the napkins are formed linear, separate designs such as palm-trees and little women. In the center, a symbolic, richly decorated cross often covered the whole central area of the cloth. The edges of the fabric were adorned with coloured tassels or with added crochet lace.

Phyti weaving was mainly made in the village of Phyti, hence the name, and neighbouring villages, as well as in other areas of the Pafos district. It was also employed in the Karpassia Peninsula, where it was used along the lower side of women's pantaloons, characteristic of the local traditional costume. These designs, which were very dense, were called *pefkota* (carpet-like).

Refugee from Karpassia with woven sheets she brought with her to Nicosia

Photo: Eleni Papademetriou, 1976

Today *Phyti weaving* is made on a limited scale in the Pafos area, mainly in the village of its origins. It is also made by a number of women trained by the Cyprus Handicraft Service.

Pottery making, village of Fini, nineteenth century

Photo: J.P Foscolo, c.1890

Pottery

Pottery-making in Cyprus is an old craft, going as far back as the Neolithic Age.

The fame of the island's pottery and *pitharia* (giant earthenware jars used in the past to store and transport wine, vinegar, oil or water),

Preparation of clay for the traditional pottery of Fini   **Photo: Cyprus Handicraft Centre**

reached Europe as early as 1394.

Until the 1974 Turkish invasion, the heart of the island's pottery industry were the villages of Fini, Kornos, Lapithos, Ayios Dimitrios, Kaminaria and the Famagusta area. Today, however, pottery-making is limited mainly to Kornos and Fini.

The soils in the area of Fini have been dug up for centuries by the villagers, who produced *pitharia* on the spot before transporting them to other areas. Fini is also famous for its intricately sculptured

Traditional pots

Replicas of amphora craters after an original of Bichrome *ware IV (1050-500 B.C.)*
Photo: Cyprus Handicraft Centre

small clay vases of a distinctive red hue. These are made by hand mostly by women without the help even of a potter's wheel and are used mainly for decoration.

The village of Kornos has managed to preserve the tradition of pottery-making, for which it is known. The shape, size and type of pottery made are according to the use they will have. Besides *pitharia*, there are the *kouzes* (medium-sized water pots), *satzia* (big, open pots for frying), *bodithes* (jug-like forms for serving water or wine) and others. Today, pottery making is preserved as a cottage industry.

The characteristics of the traditional pottery of Lapithos (in the occupied Keryneia area) are the coating known as *badanas*, the written, sprinkled or engraved decoration and the colourless glazed coating. The refugee Keryneia potters have set up their workshops again in the free areas of Cyprus where they continue the tradition.

Traditional Famagusta pottery includes mainly white pots, fired in wood-fired kilns, used as decorative pots, water jugs, crocks, or moneyboxes. They were also exported to neighbouring countries. The anthromorphic vessels of this area, which have their origins in antiquity, are of particular interest.

Traditional pottery making at Kornos   **Photo: Cyprus Handicraft Centre**

Basketry

Basket-making is one of the oldest handicrafts and has been going on for generations without any significant changes.

Cyprus' natural resources always provide suitable raw material in abundance. Very few tools are needed and used by craftsmen to make the wide variety of baskets in different shapes and sizes suitable for many uses.

The variety of materials used gives the natural colour to the items, which vary according to the mood of the maker. In some cases the raw material is dyed with bright colours. The colours used in the past were natural but today chemical colours are used.

The need for gathering and carrying goods such as potatoes, grapes, olives, fruit and so on led to the creation of items to be used for this purpose. Plaited strips of rushes, reeds or leaves of date palms were used to make soft baskets for the commercial transportation of crops or for domestic purposes. The same materials were also used to cover the roofs of sheds.

Out of all the raw material used, the easiest to find is the hard reed. It is also the easiest to use, because when soaked in water it becomes quite flexible. Furthermore, it comes in different sizes and lengths.

Different types of baskets made out of hard reed are found in villages such as Liopetri, Troulli, Mesoyi and others. These baskets are used mainly for transporting potatoes and other cultivated products.

In some cases, thin flexible twigs from trees or bushes, such as turpentine tree, monks' tree and wild olive tree are used together with the hard reed. In some villages they make different shapes of baskets using only twigs. They also use twigs to dress large glass containers, protecting them in this way from breaking, and the contents from light. The big baskets are used mainly for carrying grapes, while the glass containers for storing olive oil, wine and *zivania*, a local spirit.

Apart from cane, raw materials that are still used today are the different kinds of rushes such as *jancus acutus, erianthus*, cat's tail or

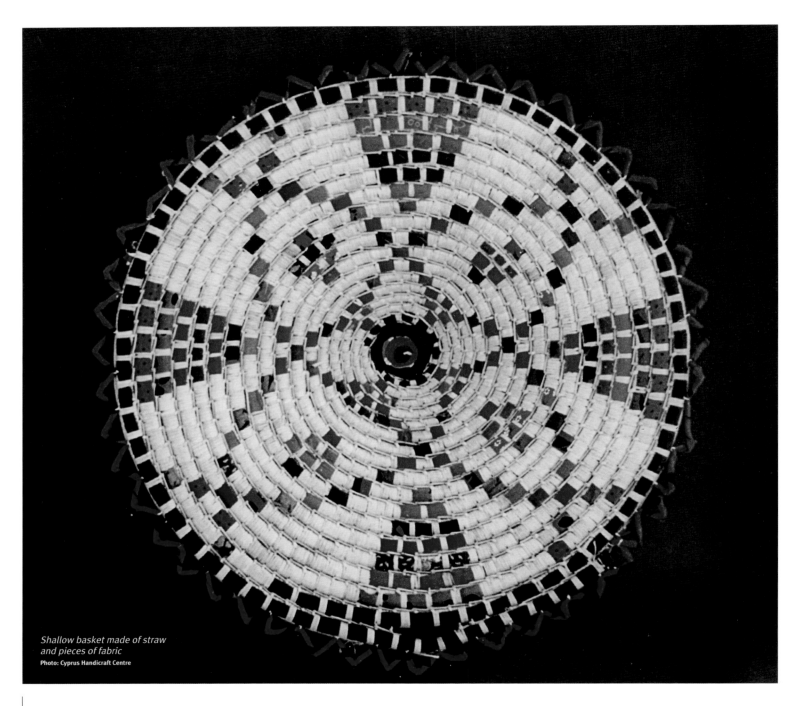

*Shallow basket made of straw
and pieces of fabric*
Photo: Cyprus Handicraft Centre

Traditional handcrafted baskets

Photo: Christos Violaris

Women learning the technique of making baskets with cane

Photo: Cyprus Handicraft Centre

club rush for carrying delicate crops. Large baskets, *farti*, were used mainly for carrying light products and *zembilia* for the olive crops. The double baskets, *sirizes*, were placed on donkeys and were used for carrying salt from the lakes, and the long strap *zembili*, slung over the left shoulder of the farmer, was used for sowing the seeds in the fields. The workers carried their olives and cheese for lunch in small lidded baskets called *korokolios*. The bread was kept in a *tapatzia* (soft basket with a cord) hanging from the ceiling in the kitchen. The *talaria* (type of soft baskets), widely used even today, are for draining and pressing Cyprus cheeses.

Palm leaves, rope from stubble and straw, were also used for making a variety of items. The technique employed for the use of these materials developed in the areas of the Karpassia Peninsula and Messaoria (now occupied areas), and spread to most of the villages as far as Pafos, where even today they make the coloured *tsestoi* (large, round flat baskets) using pieces of brightly coloured fabrics instead of coloured straw. *Tsestoi* were always used in the homes to dry in the sun local foods, such as *phides* (type of noodles) and *trachanas* (raw form of food made of wheat and milk), to keep the bread and *flaounes* (Easter cheese pies), and most importantly to carry the *koulouria* (type of bread) used as invitations for weddings and to exhibit the bride's dowry during wedding celebrations. *Tsestoi* as well as corn dollies made of straw were used to decorate houses.

Woodcarving, Cyprus Handicraft Centre

Photo: Press and Information Office

Examples of woodcarving from the Cyprus Handicraft Centre experimental workshop
Photo: Cyprus Handicraft Centre

Woodcarving

Craftsmen at different periods used wood to create a form of language to give expression to their view of the world around them, drawing their inspiration from the plant and animal kingdoms. Abstraction and symbolism produced decorative patterns which, together with geometric motifs and shapes, have resulted in amazing compositions.

The basic symbols in Cyprus woodcarving are birds (symbolising love), wolves and lions (symbolising strength), the Holy Cross (symbolising the cycle of life), and angels (symbolising guardians and protectors).

Cyprus woodcarving is divided into two categories, ecclesiastical and secular.

The iconostasis at Ayios Neophytos Monastery

Wood carved chest
Photo: Cyprus Handicraft Centre

Handmade chair with incised carved and painted decoration, after an original from the Cyprus Folk Art Museum
Photo: Cyprus Handicraft Centre

Ecclesiastical woodcarving flourished at the beginning of the sixteenth century, when the tall, carved wooden iconostasis was established in the Church of Cyprus. Examples of dynamic expressions in wood can be seen carved on iconostases, despotic thrones, pulpits, candelabras, church pews, doors.

Secular woodcarving is further divided into two categories, urban and rural. Urban woodcarving includes all types of wood furniture, such as wardrobes, tables and chairs, used by people in towns.

The main characteristic of rural woodcarving is its effortless way of expression, the lack of proportion and simplicity. Examples of this type of woodcarving are found on chests, beds, chairs, shelves, wardrobes, mirrors, etc.

The quality of the raw materials used and the degree of ornamentation and motifs employed on these objects were variously determined by the owner's social status and place of origin. The basic kinds of timber used were pine, walnut and cypress. Wood was also used for agricultural and household tools and equipment, such as ploughs, pestles and mortars, bread moulds, troughs, pack-saddles, cross-bars, looms, and shovels.

World volleyball championship, Kition stadium, Larnaka, 26.03.2004

Photo: Press and Information Office

The new stadium of the Nicosia Gymnastic club "Pagkypria"
Photo: Cyprus Sport Organisation

Sports

The sports history of Cyprus dates back many centuries. Inscriptions found in various archeological sites both on the island and in Greece bear witness to the Cypriots' love for sports, and to their success in Pan-Hellenic and Olympic contests of ancient times at Olympia, Pythia, Isthmia and elsewhere.

This is further attested by the ancient stadia of Cyprus at Kourion, Salamis(*), Pafos, Kition and Lapithos(*) which existed until the Byzantine Period. Evidence shows that during the Middle Ages athletics remained a favourite Cypriot pastime.

The first athletic club was founded in Limassol in 1897. Then similar clubs began to spring up across the island. Today, there are six major clubs operating on the island, one for each of the major towns, namely, Nicosia, Limassol, Famagusta, Larnaka, Keryneia and Pafos.

In the year 2000, 45 000 athletes of all ages were registered in 35 federations and 600 athletic clubs. These figures changed in 2004 to 60 000 athletes registered in 42 federations.

Municipal Olympic swimming pool, Larnaka

Photo: Cyprus Sport Organisation

Cyprus Sport Organisation

In its effort to promote sports, the government of Cyprus set up in 1969 the Cyprus Sport Organisation (CSO). The CSO is responsible for a wide range of activities, including supervision of out-of-school sports, financing the construction and maintenance of sports facilities, giving technical assistance to clubs and supporting participation in international competitions. Its funds are used for assisting financially the federations and clubs for the promotion of their athletic programmes, for the creation, maintenance and running of the basic athletic infrastructure (stadiums, indoor halls, sport facilities, equipment), to the highest possible standards and for the

repayment of the financial obligations of the organisation. CSO's programme "Sports for All" has been running throughout the country and is available at 180 sports centres.

The CSO runs sports centres, Olympic-standard swimming pools and multi-use indoor halls across the island. One such facility is the multi-purpose indoor hall Eleftheria, which facilitates practice and competition in almost every sport.

With assistance from the CSO, the Nicosia Squash Club has initiated a training programme for school age children. Already, some of its

Olympic flame welcome ceremony, Kimon square, Larnaka, 09.07.2005

graduates are among the sport's best, representing Cyprus in international competitions.

In 2000 the new stadium of the Pankypria Nicosia Athletic Club, which consists of one football stadium seating 25 000 spectators, one track and field stadium seating 2 000 spectators and another field with track opened for use. The stadium is one of the most modern in Europe providing every facility needed by athletes, journalists and spectators.

In view of new trends in world sports, the CSO has been successfully running a Centre for Sports Research, whose purpose is to assist athletes in all fields to excel at international competitions. The Centre cooperates with other similar centres in Europe.

Cyprus Olympic Committee

In the year 2003, the Cyprus Olympic Committee celebrated twenty-five years of affiliation with the International Olympic Committee.

With the Athens 2004 Olympic Games, the focus of the Committee was on the preparation and support of the Olympic team. Financial, technical and psychological support for the athletes were part of the Committee's multi-faceted "Olympic Preparation Plan". Reward came

Children's activities at the Olympic Day Run

Cypriot swimmer Karolina Pelendritou, gold medal winner in the Women's 100m Breaststroke – SB13 at the Athens 12th Paraolympic Games, 25.09.2004   Photo: Athens News Agency

in the person of Cypriot swimmer Karolina Pelendritou, who won Cyprus' first-ever Olympic gold medal at the Athens 2004 Paraolympic Games.

Perhaps the most ambitious project that the Cyprus Olympic Committee has undertaken is the construction of the Olympic House and Park, the heart of sport and Olympism in Cyprus. The Olympic House and Park is home, not only to the Cyprus Olympic Committee, but also to its forty-two national member-Federations.

Ta Hassamboulia *(Vendetta)*,
by Costas Demetriou
Photo: Costas Demetriou

Cinema

The cinematographic production in a small country like Cyprus had an inevitable late start and a rather slow development in its early years.

The history of cinema in Cyprus begins at the end of the 1940s, when the British colonial government started to train Cypriot film makers at the Colonial Film Unit. And with the advent of Cypriot television in 1957, the first short-length films, mainly documentaries, began to be made.

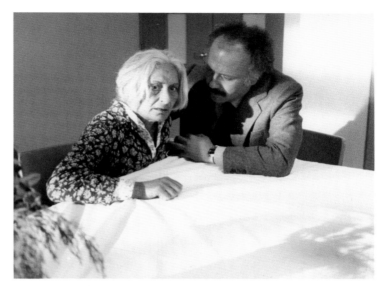

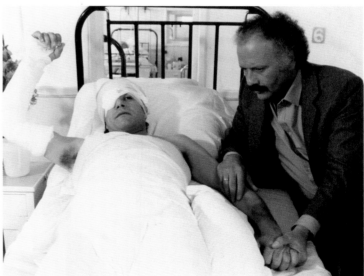

The Rape of Aphrodite, *by Andreas Pantzis, first prize, Salonica Film Festival 1985*

Photo: Andreas Pantzis

Ta Hassamboulia *(Vendetta), by Costas Demetriou*

Photo: Costas Demetriou

The pioneers of Cypriot cinema during the 1950s were George Lanitis, Ninos Fenek Mikellides, Renos Watson, Polys Georgakis and others who directed and produced short-length films. Some of these were: *The Island of Aphrodite, Salamina, Botrys of Cyprus, Epikoinonia* (Communication) and *Rizes* (Roots) of Nikos Lanitis and George Stivaros, who run the independent production company Aphrodite. The first film of this company was *To Heri* (The hand).

I Sfagi tou Kokora *(The Slaughter of the Cock), by Andreas Pantzis, prize for direction,*
Salonica Film Festival 1996   Photo: Andreas Pantzis

Feature-length films were produced much later in the 1960s. George
Filis in 1963 directed a film depicting the traditional Cypriot wedding,
in 1965 *Agapes kai Kaimoi* (Love affairs and Heartbreaks) and soon
after *To Telefteo Fili* (The last kiss), 1821 and *Cyprus*. In 1969 Foto-
Cine (George Katsouris and Costas Farmakas) directed the comedy *O
Paras o Maskaras* (Money the Clown).

During the late 60s and early 70s there was a richer crop of films.
George Filis produced and directed *Gregoris Afxentiou, Etsi*

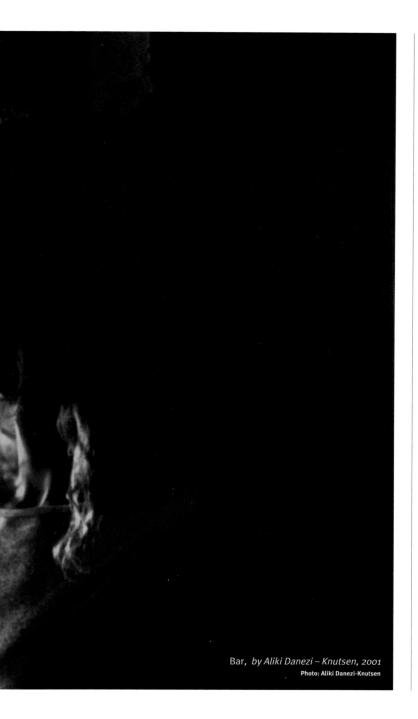

Bar, *by Aliki Danezi – Knutsen, 2001*

Photo: Aliki Danezi-Knutsen

Kato apo ta Astra *(Under the Stars), by Christos Georgiou, 2001, Prix de Montreal,Best First Feature*

Photo: Christos Georgiou

Prodothike I Kypros (Cyprus' Betrayal), and the *Mega Document.* The cinematographic entrepreneur D. Herodotou also started producing films: *Dakrya kai Diplopenies* (Tears and Strings), *I Diki tou Fitilla* (Fitillas' Trial), *I Apagogi tis Gogous* (Kidnapping Gogou), *O Firfiris stin Athena* (Firfiris visits Athens), *To Ftohopedo tis Kyprou* (The Cypriot pauper), *Diakopes stin Kypro* (Holidaying in Cyprus) and *O Tragoudistis tis Kyprou* (The Cyprus Singer).

In the mid and late 70s Costas Demetriou produced and directed a number of feature films: *Ta Hassamboulia* (Vendetta), *Skotoste ton Makario* (Order to Kill Makarios) and *Gia pion na Vrexi* (For whom should it rain?).

In 1985 Christos Shopahas was awarded first prize at the Moscow Festival for his film *The Descent of the Nine*.

In the 80s the following feature films were also produced: *O Avrianos Polemistis* (Tomorrow's Warrior) by Michalis Papas, *Trimithi*, *O Viasmos tis Afroditis* (The rape of Aphrodite) by Andreas Panztis, that won first prize at the Salonica Festival in 1985, and *Nekatomenoi Aerides* (Troubled Winds) by Yiannis Ioannou.

The most recent productions include: *To Ftero tis Migas* (The Wing of the Fly) by Cypriot Director Christos Shopahas (it won the prize for direction at the Salonica Festival in 1995), *I Sfagi tou Kokora* (The Slaughter of the Cock) by Andreas Panztis (it won the prize for direction at the Salonica Festival in 1996) and *Dromoi kai Portokalia* (Roads and Oranges) by Aliki Danezi Knutsen (1997). *I Sfagi tou Kokora*, a Cypriot-Greek-Bulgarian co-production, was nominated by Greece as its representative in the Oscar awards for best foreign language film for 1997.

Cinematographic production in Cyprus received a boost in May 1994 when the Council of Ministers established the Cinema Advisory Committee. The committee comprises government officials and representatives from the private sector, i.e., producers, directors and some celebrities from the cinema sector appointed directly by the Council of Ministers. The committee is mandated to recommend for funding to a competent ministerial committee the best proposals submitted by Cypriot producers/directors in the categories of feature-length films, short films and documentaries. The committee also encourages co-productions with other countries. Finally, it has the responsibility to study in depth the situation of cinema in Cyprus and make suggestions for the enactment of legislation governing all matters related to cinematography and in general audiovisual works on the island.

The Road to Ithaca, *by Costas Demetriou, 1997*
Photo: Costas Demetriou

IACA

Since its establishment and after it decided on the criteria, the basic requirements and conditions for the submissions of projects, as well as the procedures to be followed, the committee allocated financial support for almost seventy films.

The most recent productions include: *Kai to Treno Paei ston Ourano* (And the Train goes to the Sky) by Ioannis Ioannou (2000); *To Tama* (The Promise) by Andreas Pantzis; *Kato apo ta astra* (Under the Stars) by Christos Georgiou; and *Bar* by Aliki Danezi-Knusten (all in 2001).

In 2001, Christos Georgiou received the Prix de Montreal (Best First Feature) for his film *Under the Stars* at the International World Film Festival in Montreal. In the same year he also received the following honours for the same film: (1) Best First Feature at the Twentieth International Film Festival in Montevideo, Uruguay; (2) the Special Award of the International Cinema Critics FIPRESCI, Montevideo, Uruguay; (3) Gold Award for Foreign Feature Film at the Houston Film Festival; (4) the Gold Special Jury Award Gold REMI for Foreign Feature Film at the Houston Film Festival; and (5) the Granada Audience Award for Best Feature Film at the Manchester Commonwealth Film Festival.

In 2001 Andreas Pantzis' film *To Tama* won at the 42nd Salonica Film Festival the following awards: (1) the Special Award of the International Cinema Critics FIRESCI as the best Greek Film; (2) the third award of the Best Greek Film given by the Greek Ministry of Culture; and (3) Best Male Lead Performance award. Finally, Ioannis Ioannou's film *Kai to Treno Paei ston Ourano* received the award of best photography at the 2nd Mediterranean Film Festival in Cologne.

Two other Cypriot films won top honours at international festivals. The documentary *Beyond Division* received the Special Jury Award at the 35th WorldFest International Film Festival held in Houston, Texas, (2002) following in the footsteps of the documentary *Unwitnessed Memories*, which won the same award at the 34th WorldFest International Film Festival. *Unwitnessed Memories*, directed by Athena Xenidou, expolores how the younger generation in Cyprus perceives the 1974 Turkish invasion.

Beyond Division is a production of the Press and Information Office of the Republic of Cyprus in collaboration with the American film company Peter Vogt and Associates Inc. It won the 35th World Fest International Film Festival's category of "Political and International

To Tama (Evagoras' Vow) by Andreas Pantzis, Special Award of the International Cinema Critics FIRESCI as the best Greek film, Salonica Film Festival 2001

Photo: Andreas Pantzis

invasion of Turkey in 1974. A festival press release refers to "the exceptional excellence of the film" and says that the "stunning scenes of Cyprus and its people today, as well as the fascinating and dramatic historical imagery is brought together with compelling contemporary interviews with journalists, statesmen and Cypriot citizens who have endured the tragic division of their island state."

Beyond Division, Special Jury Award, 35th World Fest International Film Festival, Houston, Texas

Photo: Press and Information Office

Issues" among 3 900 entries. It was also selected as one of the finalists for the festival's highest award among all the film and video productions, an award it won. *Beyond Division* also won an award for Best International Newsworthy Documentary Film, at the 9th International Film Festival Cinevue held in Bostwick, Florida.

The half-hour documentary unfolds the story of Cyprus from its earliest history to its contemporary reality, as a result of the military

Furthermore, a Cypriot-made short film, *Mavroscoufitsa* (Little Black Riding Hood), written and directed by Yiannis Yiapanis and produced by Elmos K. Neocleous, was honoured at the Cannes Film Festival. The film, a Cypriot-Italian co-production of the Cyprus Cinema Advisory Committee and Lumiere Service and Zootroupe Productions, was filmed on location in Limassol, Cyprus. It is a portrayal of the subconscious mind of Little Red Riding Hood, through criticisms of the fairy tale's symbolic explanation.

Little Black Riding Hood was one of eleven films selected for screening at that year's Cannes Festival out of 1 340 short films submitted. This was quite an accomplishment for Cyprus, since it was the first time that a Cypriot film had been accepted for this category at the festival.

In 2003, the following films were released: *Barea Anthygiena* by Antonis Papadopoulos, *Kalabush* by Adonis Florides and Theodoros Nicolaides, and *Red Thursday* by Christos Shopahas. In 2004, the documentary *Cyprus: Legendary, magical and thoroughly modern* was released. The 45-minute film by Kurt W. Oehlschlager and Klaus Gallas, a co-production of Amara Filmproduktion and the Press and Information Office, is a description and reflection of all that makes up modern Cyprus, her customs and traditions, her natural features, her churches, her culture, all of these always in conjunction with and as a continuation of her ancient-old civilisation and troubled history.

Since 2004, the Press and Information Office, in cooperation with various production companies, has produced 34 short documentaries on various aspects of life in Cyprus. In addition, since 2004, the Cyprus Cinema Archives, under the Press and Information Office, has introduced an innovative programme of filming all towns and villages in Cyprus.

The Eurimages Fund

Cyprus was one of the founding members of the Eurimages Fund, a Council of Europe initiative, in 1989. As a result, Cypriot co-productions are eligible for funding from the Eurimages Fund, which is, *inter alia*, financing European film co-productions. To date, five feature-length films in which Cyprus was the major co-producer have received funding from Eurimages.

The first was *I Sfagi tou Kokora* (Slaughter of the Cock) of Andreas Pantzis (1992), which has been completed in 1996, *Kai to Traino Paei ston Ourano* (And the Train goes to the Sky) (1994) of Yiannis Ioannou, completed in 2000, *O Dromos pros tin Ithaki* (The Road to Ithaca) (1997) of Costas Demetriou, completed in 1999, and *To Tama* (The Promise) (1999) of Andreas Pantzis, completed in 2001. The latest feature films which received funding by Eurimages are Adonis Florides' *Kalabush* and Panicos Chrysanthou's *Akamas*.

In addition, *To Ftero tis Migas* (Wing of the Fly) of Cypriot director Christos Shopachas and *Vysinokipos* (Cherry Orchard), an adaptation of Chekhov's play by Cypriot-born director, Michael Kakoyiannis, have received funding from Eurimages with Greece as the major co-producer. In total, Cyprus has participated as a coproducer in the production of fifteen feature-length films funded by Eurimages, with a total subsidy from the fund of nearly three million euro.

Participation in the Media Plus Programme

In February 2003, Cyprus signed in Brussels a Memorandum of Understanding with the European Union ensuring its participation in the Media Plus Programme (2001-2005), which is the sequel to the Media II Programme. Cyprus had been participating in the Media II Programme since 1999. For the year 2003, Cyprus contributed 240 000 euro to the Programme budget, thereby entitling Cypriot professionals access to all initiatives of the Nicosia Media Desk, which has been in operation since July 2003. Cyprus has been participating in the Media Committees, overseeing the funding process with two Cypriot members having observer status.

The status of Cyprus in the Media Plus Programme changed in May 2004 when it acceded to the European Union. Its participation is now funded from its overall contribution to the Community budget, whereas it participates in the Media Committee as a full member. The island's participation in the program is overseen by the Press and Information Office of the Ministry of Interior.

Kissonerghis Ioannis
(1889-1963)
Turk with Narghile,
watercolour, 1945-48,
34x16 cm

Century of Visual Arts

The creation of visual arts in the recent and contemporary history of Cypriot art has followed its own course which was different from that of Western Europe. After three centuries of cultural isolation as a result of Ottoman rule, the island experienced its first cultural awakening in the period before World War I. The socio-economic and political changes that took place gradually created conditions for the surfacing of expressions of art other than Byzantine and folk art.

The pioneers of this awakening were: the poet Vassilis Michaelides; prose writers Nicos Nicolaides and Vassilis Vryonides; Andreas Thymopoulos, the first Cypriot who formally studied art; and Ioannis Kissonerghis, the most important artistic presence during the early part of the century.

These artists paved the way for a second generation of artists who, with their more fundamental quests, laid the foundations of contemporary Cypriot art. These artists are Adamantios Diamantis, George Pol. Georghiou, Solomos Frangoulides, Victor Ioannides, Loukia Nicolaidou-Vassiliou and Telemachos Kanthos. All of them, except the self-taught Georghiou, completed their studies at schools of fine arts abroad and on their return to Cyprus engaged themselves systematically in artistic creativity.

Their creativity is inspired by experience, while their subjects are drawn from the natural and human environment, from daily life and historical events. They rendered these through various representational artistic vocabularies, each artist developing his/her own personal morphoplastic language.

When Cyprus won its independence, conditions for creating and promoting art started to improve: the creation of a cultural department within the Ministry of

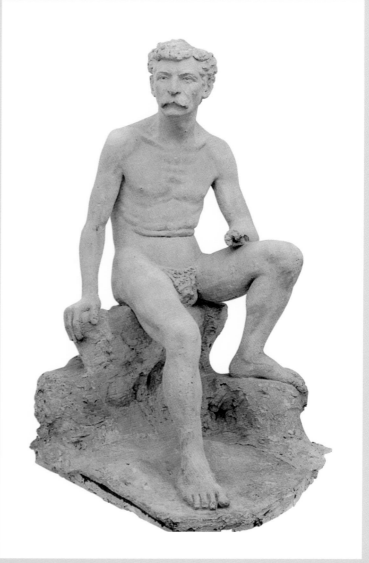

Thymopoulos Andreas (1881-1953)
Ulysses nostalgic, *plaster, 1908, 95x68x96 cm*

Diamantis Adamantios (1900-1994) Asmaalti Coachmen, *oil, 1943, 61x82 cm*

Education was the beginning of the gradual institutionalisation of the State's interest in the arts and letters. Consequently, artistic activity intensified, and the curiosity of society was kindled. At the same time, the opportunity given from the late 1960s to many Cypriot artists to participate in international art exhibitions and biennale brought about an international visibility and the gradual emergence of the hitherto isolated Cypriot art.

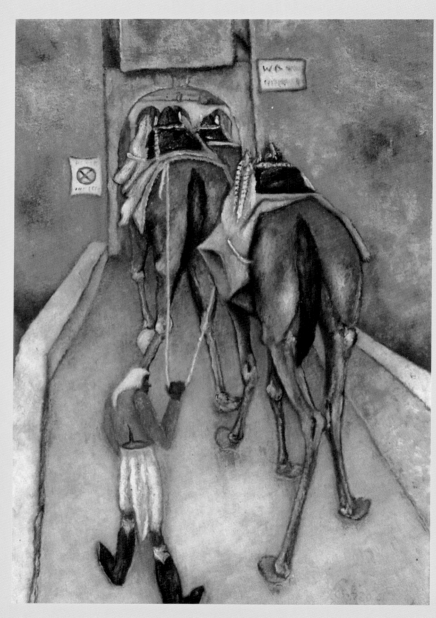

Georghiou Pol. George
Camels at Famagusta
Gate, 1951,
oil, 62 x 42 cm.

Frangoulides Solomos (1902-1981) Little Rock in the Sea, *acrylic, 1973, 50x60 cm*

Nicolaidou-Vassiliou Loukia
(1909-1994)
Enosis, a Dream of Cyprus, *oil,*
between 1954-1956, 137x111 cm

The number of Cypriots studying art has increased noticeably. As early as the 1950s, a small number of young artists who had completed their studies abroad, especially in Britain, began to return to Cyprus. The number of such artists increased substantially during the 1960s.

These artists studied art in the major centres of Europe, where they experienced first hand the intense and multifarious fermentation which broadened the field of artistic activity, renewed its content and enriched its forms and its language. They were naturally infused by this new spirit and the questing attitude towards art. Through their work that embraced the new currents, they contributed to the gradual harmonisation of Cyprus with international artistic developments.

An important figure of this generation and the first to return to Cyprus was Christophoros Savva, who forms the link between the art which developed on the island before and after Independence. Before the end of the 1960s, an additional group of dynamic artists returned to Cyprus and worked to secure the dominance of the values of abstract art. Either obeying some inner need or inspired by some external subject, artists such as Andreas Chrysochos, Stelios Votsis,

Telemachos Kanthos (1910-1993)
In the Yard, *oil, 1980, 61x45 cm*

Christoforos Savva *(1924-1968)* Still life, *oil, 1959, 66x81 cm*

Christoforos Savva *(1924-1968)*
Abstract sculpture, stone,
68x37x33 cm

Stelios Votsis The Cyclist, *acrylic, 1987, 85x85 cm*

Kate Stephanidou, Vera Hadjida, Marios Loizides, Nicos Kouroussis, Andreas Ladommatos, Costas Ioacheim and others expressed themselves in the abstract artistic language which marked Cypriot art of this period.

Cypriot sculpture followed the same quests within contemporary trends during the first period after independence. Using abstract and geometrical vocabularies and in the spirit of constructivism, neoplasticism and also contemporary English sculpture, a number of young sculptors, such as Demetris Constantinou, Andreas Savvides and George Sfikas, concentrated their attention on three-dimensional geometrical forms and on the potential of material, giving emphasis to tectonic elements. Constantinou also produced some works of kinetic art, while Andis Hadjiadamos worked with biomorphic shapes, which had, as their starting point, the organic world and the human form.

Toward the end of the sixties and the beginning of the seventies, vocabularies of expression were enriched through such artists as Glyn Hughes, Andreas Charalambides, Constantinos Yiannicouris, John Corbidge, George Kotsonis and others. Angelos Makrides and George Sfikas took important steps in minimalising their means of expression and turning their attention to conceptual art. They were also the first artists to work on installations in space.

The tragic experience of the Turkish invasion and its national, political, economic and social aftermath could not fail to influence the natural course of contemporary Cypriot art. The artist who has a direct relationship with historic events inevitably links his/her work to the historic present. Some artists, in their efforts to communicate through more easily comprehensible messages, resort to realistic forms of expression, while others insert representational themes among abstract motifs, often with symbolic projections. Generally, symbolism, either of colour or shape, and expressionistic traits characterise many of the works of the post-1974 period. The long

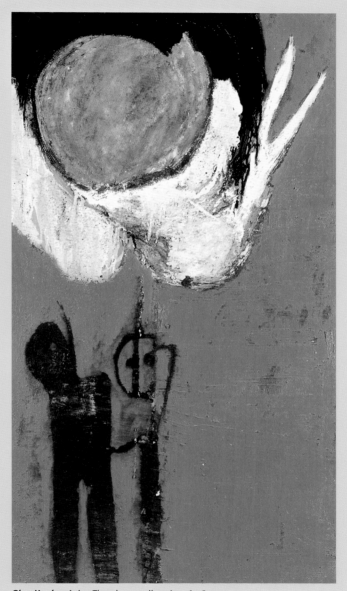

Glyn Hughes Ayios Theodoros, *oil, 1962, 161x87 cm*

Nicos Kouroussis
Surpassing,
*mixed media, 1986,
180x180 cm*

Gregoriou Theodoulos Historical Landscape, *mixed media, 1992*

Painter *Keti Stefanidou*

continuation of the Cypriot political crisis, which intensified the need to preserve ethnic identities and features, together with the value crisis that affects art on an international level and the reevaluation of national specificities, forced many artists to go back to the sources of their own space, giving life to creative symbols and artistic memories.

The closer we come to the present day the more difficult it becomes to approach the forms of contemporary Cypriot art objectively, because our view of its aesthetic directions and ideological orientations is not complete. Nevertheless, we can make some general statements, distinguish some directions or recognise some individual artistic records which, by being of outstanding dynamism and truth, constitute, at the same time, important achievements and points of departure.

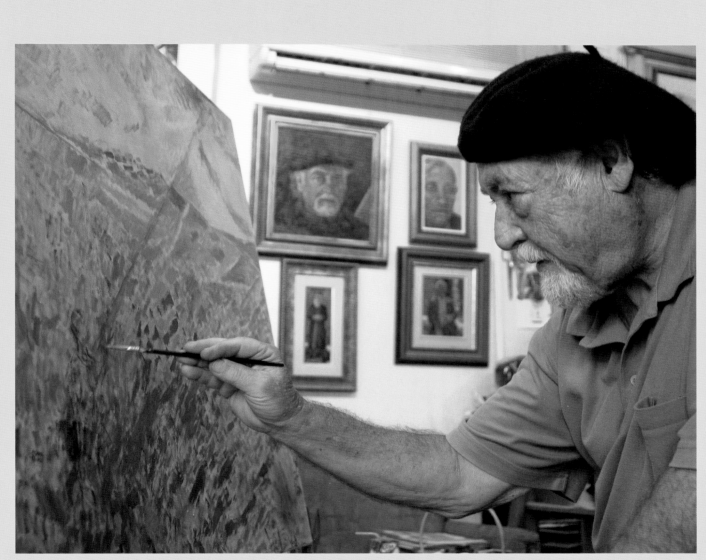

*Painter **Lefteris Economou***

Maria Loizidou
Summaries,
Sculptures, Drawings,
mixed media, 1989,
*90x40x30 cm., 210x22x12
cm., 170x22x12 cm*

Lefteris Economou Roofs in Nicosia, *oil, 1956, 54x75 cm*

Yannicouris Constantinos
Tree gazing out of the Window, *oil, 1957, 150x130 cm*

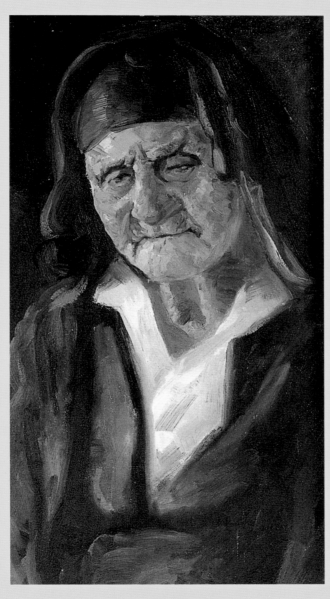

Costas Averkiou
My Mother, *oil, 1958, 66x35 cm*

George Kotsonis
Nude, *acrylic, 1978,*
85x75 cm

Paraskos Stass Pagan Spring, *oil, 1968, 143x210 cm*

Michael Kashalos Reaping and Eating, *oil, 969, 72x102 cm*

Indisputably, the chief characteristic of the 1980s was the multiplicity of stylistic and morphoplastic directions. The absence of a school of fine arts in Cyprus compels Cypriots to study art abroad. Britain no longer has the monopoly on Cypriot students who, since the middle of the 1960s, have been studying in ever-increasing numbers in Greece, France, Italy, Russia and other countries, particularly countries of Eastern Europe. Thus, they developed artistically in a variety of aesthetic and philosophical climates, embarking on their artistic course from different starting points. Furthermore, they are no longer isolated as before. With distances becoming globally shorter and shorter and with opportunities to participate in international exhibitions, the Cypriot artist has access to information and knowledge about the trends that predominate internationally and can place his/her own quests more easily within the international artistic spirit. These exogenous factors are counterbalanced by the power the Cypriot land exerts on the artists. The dialogue between the exogenous and endogenous factors is conducted for each artist at a personal level, and determines the polymorphism which characterises contemporary Cypriot art as it appears in the 1980s.

Hakeri Yilmaz Casino Akar,
oil, 1972, 83x57 cm

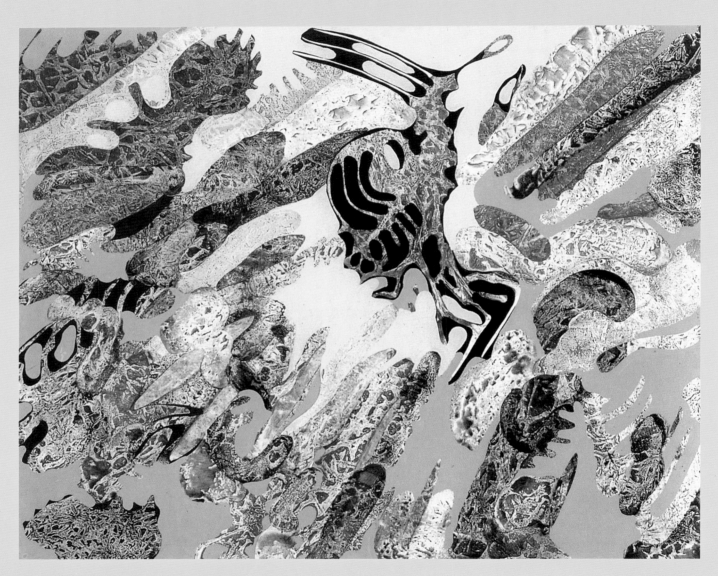

George Skotinos Landscape, *acrylic, 1967, 102x126 cm*

Andreas Makariou
Meze at Kato Pafos,
oil, 1983, 140x122 cm

Andreas Charalambous Full moon over New York, *oil, 1983-84, 76x102 cm*

Another trend that we see crystallising with ever-increasing clarity is the relationship between artistic creation and the very destiny of the island, which intervenes actively and influences the young artists to a greater or lesser extent. The trials and tribulations of the country, the day-to-day sense of insecurity and suspense, the waiting and the uncertain tomorrow which they experience at a conscious or unconscious level, and which is reinforced by other pessimistic universal messages, create a spiritual anguish which is reflected in their creations, particularly those of younger artists, as existential agony or as a dialogue between life and death.

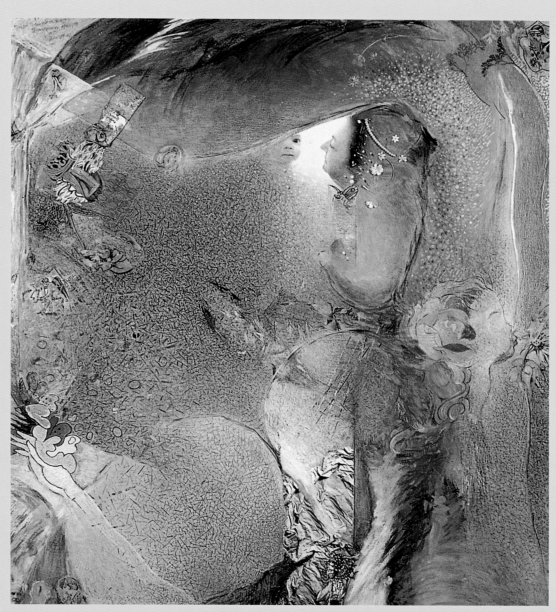

Ioannides Andreas-Antis
Dense Soul, *mixed
media, 1987, 101x101 cm*

Christos Foukaras The Dragon, *tempera, 1995, 65x79 cm*

Painter **Christos Foukaras**

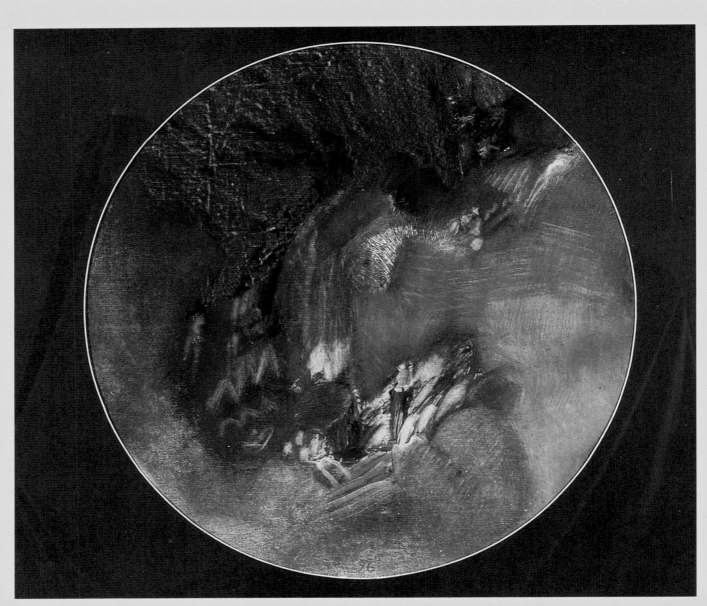

Rhea Bailey Earth of Volcanoes, *oil, 1996,diam. 51 cm*

Christos Christou
Portrait of an Angel, *2000,*
acrylic, 68χ48 cm

Maria Perentou
Whiteness, *2002*,
acrylic, 147X90 cm

Eleni Nikodemou Dance of the Angels, *2003, acrylic, 200χ200 cm*

Lia Vogiazi,
Ready or not, *2003,*
oil, 200 x113 cm

This trend links Cypriot art with some dominant forms of contemporary international art, which do not want artistic creation to be isolated but which involve it in a wider spectrum and transform it into reader, theoretician, expounder, poet and exorciser of the present and omen for the future.

Artistic language is being renewed and broadened continuously. From the mid-1980s several artists have shown a particular preference for the exploration of the potential of materials and for the energy which the work of art creates. Thus, we have an increasing number of constructions and installations in space.

There are, however, some young artists who remain faithful to the values of painting and the two-dimensional picture. With various gestures and vocabularies which reveal their constant contact with what is happening in art worldwide, they produce their own mythologies.

Thanks to its creative robustness, Cypriot art has managed to assert itself and cover a lot of ground in just a few decades, in order to articulate a valuable artistic language.

Melita Kouta
Objects of Desire,
2005, mixed media